Praise for Leeny's Fight

"I have been gifted a friendship and have been inspired by Eileen and her work advocating for and shedding light on pediatric cancer. Her book is the journey not only through the physical but the mental challenges the disease brings. I have personally witnessed this amazing growth with my own eyes! There is positive life after cancer, and Eileen brings it to the forefront!"

—**Glenn Davis**, Former Professional Soccer Player, Nationally Recognized Broadcaster, Soccer Matters, ESPN Radio

"This is a compelling account of Eileen's epic battle against childhood cancer and the mental struggles that ensued. Follow this story of redemption as it unfolds, and she finds meaning and purpose after the storm. Her words will pierce your heart."

—**Kristi Wilkinson**, Adoption Advocate and Author, *The Child Who Listens*

LEENY'S FIGHT

A MEMOIR OF A CHILDHOOD CANCER SURVIVOR

EILEEN DOWD

LEENY'S FIGHT
A Memoir of a Childhood Cancer Survivor

ISBN: 978-1-08-799865-7 (Paperback)
ISBN: 978-1-08-799871-8 (ebook)

Printed in the United States of America

TABLE OF CONTENTS

PROLOGUE

Every three minutes, a family is devastated by the news that their child has been diagnosed with some form of cancer. Approximately 1 in 285 children in the United States will be diagnosed with cancer before their twentieth birthday. Each year in the United States, an estimated 15,780 children between birth and nineteen years old will be diagnosed with a form of cancer. Globally there are more than 300,000 children diagnosed with cancer each year.[1]

There are two battles when it comes to pediatric cancer. Battle number one, fight like hell and survive. Battle number two, survive the mental toll of beating cancer as you grow older. You see, for me, beating cancer was the easy part. Life after cancer, being called a survivor, was the true test of my mental state. Unfortunately, studies show that children diagnosed with cancer before the age of ten tend to have a higher risk of being treated for a mental health disorder.

A wave serves as the intertwining path between each section of a person's life. Waves represent every passage of time in ways in which life changes while also staying the same. Waves represent the simultaneous individuality and connectivity of life's experiences. Ocean waves are like different situations in life, and they remind you that nothing lasts forever, such as joy and sadness. Waves come

---

1 "US Childhood Cancer Statistics," American Childhood Cancer Organization (ACCO), https://www.acco.org/us-childhood-cancer-statistics/.

crashing and never stop, even for a moment. Everything passes so quickly. Waves are one of the most potent forces of nature on earth. They also hold a certain level of duality, as they have been known to swallow you whole, but waves can also propel you to the proper destination you're meant for.

CHAPTER ONE

Calm before the Storm

My mom, Maribel, thoughtfully journaled my battle with cancer. I take that back; my mom journaled our battle with cancer. Yes, I was the one with the cancer diagnosis. But everyone in my family was also involved in this battle, especially my parents. Everyone played their part in this epic battle with my life on the line.

June 4th, 1998

The kids and I were spending two weeks in Dallas as a vacation. My sister's friend hosted us at their home, which was so lovely and relaxing to be able to take my family at the end of the day. We were able to see everyone, family and friends.

Eileen was not acting herself most of the time. She was not eating much; she was sleeping a lot, but she returned to her usual "Leeny" self again. Over the past few days, she ran a slight fever which I tried to tame down with Motrin. Everyone within our extended family was beginning to notice a change in Eileen. She just was not her usual talkative self, and I just assumed she might have been homesick and missing her dad.

On Thursday, June 4, 1998, the kids and I went to Aunt Carol's house for a birthday party. Aunt Carol prepared delicious cupcakes and had gifts for Eileen, Anthony, Joshua, and Jake. It was so much fun for everyone. Eileen was acting normal on this day, but not much later, Aunt Carol noticed she felt hot. I immediately took her temperature, and it was 102 degrees. It was so strange to me that she was her usual self and had been running such a high fever. I called the local doctor, and he assured me it must be some virus and suggested taking her to urgent care in Plano, Texas.

I quickly gathered our things and got ready to leave when my sister-in-law, Patty, told me to make sure I asked the doctor to do a CBC (complete blood count). When we arrived, the doctor looked at Eileen, her ears, nose, and throat. After his exam, he looked at me and said, "I do not see anything wrong with her." We paused as we looked at one another, puzzled, and I asked him to collect a CBC. The nurse soon came in and took Eileen's blood. When she turned Eileen's hand over to look at the tips of her fingers, her whole body language changed as she discovered how white the palms of Eileen's hands were. I was starting to worry. I thought about how I never checked the palms of my kid's hands. I knew it was not expected, but at that moment, I could not begin to think this could have been something serious.

About ten minutes later, the doctor walked back into our room and told me he was having the nurse run the labs a second time. By then, Eileen was asleep in my arms. Soon after, the doctor came back in and told me that Leeny's blood count was meager, and she was anemic. He then went on to say to me I needed to get her to an Emergency Room immediately. So many thoughts were running through my mind; I was not comprehending what was going on. Finally, I asked, "If I get in my car and drive her to Houston to her primary doctor would she be okay"? He responded, "No, ma'am. I am not a pediatric doctor, but if this were you, I would be giving you a blood transfusion right now." I was so worried; I was so scared. I called Aunt Carol before I left the doctor's office, and I just burst into tears, barely able to speak. She quickly told me she was on her way to me.

Aunt Carol and I drove to the Emergency Room in Plano, Texas. The team helping Eileen drew more blood and did a urine sample and a chest X-ray. By then, my in-laws Joni and Lance (Grammy and Pop-Pop) were there with us as well. Lance was trying desperately to get a hold of Eileen's dad, Pat. Pat had been in meetings all day and was on his way back to Houston for work. He was planning on flying into Dallas on Friday. At the time, the bishop from our church came by to give Eileen a blessing; I was trying so hard to stay positive.

The doctor walked in and started talking about blood counts, what they mean and how they work. By then, again, Eileen was asleep in my arms. It was close to 9:00 p.m. Aunt Carol, Joni, and I just sat there as the doctor told us Children's Hospital was already waiting for us. We all just sat there with our mouths open, staring at one another, and I finally looked at the doctor and said, "What are you telling me? What is wrong with my daughter?" He replied, "Well, ma'am, your daughter may have either a serious virus, Leukemia, or another form of cancer." I was in complete and utter shock; we all were. All I could do was sit there with my Leeny in my arms, fast asleep. As the doctor walked out of the room, I burst into tears, sobbing. I could not believe what was happening. I was shaking; all I wanted was Pat to get there already. I called my mom, Eileen's grandma. I could not even get the words out; all I could do was cry. She told me to pray to Heavenly Father, to have faith everything would be okay. I prayed the entire way to the hospital.

Pop Pop finally got a hold of Pat and was driving to the airport to pick him up. At that point, Pat had no idea what information we had just received. We stopped at Wendy's, and Eileen ate chicken nuggets and fries. Then she was fast asleep, again. We got to the Hospital. We went to the tenth floor. I remember just holding my sweet girl in my arms and just praying to God. I was so petrified for her. I lifted my head as the elevator doors opened, and there on the wall, big letters read "Cancer and Blood Disorders." Pat finally got to us that night; the doctor walked into our room and asked us questions. By that time, Eileen was already hooked up to an IV and fast asleep. He told us that they would test her bone marrow in the morning and that this test would be more definitive in what was going on. Pat and I did not sleep that night; all we could do was cry, both of us.

The doctors and team ran the bone marrow testing that following morning, and sure enough, Eileen was diagnosed with Leukemia. Again, the shock we were in was inexplainable. I cannot begin to explain the feelings, the emotions. It was almost like time stopped, and we were the *only people there; we just could not think straight at that point. Everyone within the community, our friends, and our family started calling and visiting. The phone was ringing off the hook.*

June 5, 1998

Eileen got her first blood transfusion, and bone marrow testing was done. Everything started right away. Urgent. She had fevers on and off.

June 6, 1998

We were released from the hospital to go home for our treatments. We went back to my sister's friend's house, where I bathed Eileen. She looked so skinny and fragile with bruises where the IV had been and from her finger pricks. She ate her dinner and went back to sleep. Pat and I loaded the car. Anthony, Josh, and Jake were with my mom. We stopped at Joni and Lance's house to say our goodbyes. When we arrived, Aunt Carol was there, and when she went to see Eileen, she noticed how warm she was feeling once again. I checked her temperature, and sure enough, it was 102 degrees. I immediately called the hospital back, and they asked us to come back where they administered a shot of antibiotics and did a blood culture.

After we rushed to the airport, we got on the first plane to Houston. I remember running to the terminal with my little Leeny and telling the flight attendant we had to get on that plane. She called a driver who took us to our gate. We were the last ones on the plane. Eileen had never been on an airplane before, and she was so excited but so weak. She was fast asleep before we even left the runway. She slept the entire way there. All I could do was pray and cry. When we arrived, she was still fast asleep in my arms. A family friend was there to pick us up from the Houston airport and took us immediately to Texas Children's Hospital. As I stared out the window of the car, I knew everything was about to change. Treatments were going to be administered immediately, and life as we knew it was forever going to be changed. That continuous feeling of helplessness continued to take over my mind and body. All I wanted to do was scream. How could this be happening? This must have been a terrible dream I would soon wake up from. I was wrong; all I wanted was to take this disease away from my Leeny girl.

We got to the Texas Children's emergency room. That night felt like it went on forever. One of the nurses kindly brought some activities and games for Eileen to work on. We played Candy land until at least 3:00 a.m. I remember the room being so cold, and I was just absolutely exhausted in every possible way. The next nurse we had was a male, and boy, was he a real jerk. He came into our room at 4:00 a.m.; Eileen was so tired and refused to open her mouth for him to take her temperature. He insisted on her opening her mouth, and I was beginning to get pissed off at how he was acting and treating my little girl. I grabbed my thermometer from my bag and took Eileen's temperature under her arm, and he refused to take my thermometer reading. He then went on to tell me he was going to have to take my daughter's temperature rectally. He grabbed my daughter, pulled down her pants as she was screaming, and took her temperature. I shouted over the top of Eileen's and demanded he gets the hell out of our room and never come back. The actual doctor came in, and I told him exactly what had happened and how that male nurse acted toward us, and that doctor said to me that the nurse should have never taken her temperature rectally, and you never do that with cancer patients. The rage that filled my body, I could have strangled that man. By 5:30 a.m., we made it up to the tenth floor for admission.

November 1, 1998

Today Eileen woke up sweating and thirsty; she lay on the couch in our living room and looked drained. I brought her favorite chocolate milk and soon discovered her head was wet and her face was sweating. She did not have a fever, so I called the doctor because I knew that was not normal. The doctor asked me to bring her into the hospital as Eileen may have some sort of infection she was fighting. She told me to bring an overnight bag just in case. We got ready to leave. Things happened so fast; one minute, we were home, then in the car, and then the Emergency Room. Thankfully one of the friends I made at the hospital was able to keep Anthony, Josh, and Jake for me, they were from Mexico, and their daughter was fighting Lymphoma. They were so lovely and so in need yet always were there to help support us. Their daughter Corina and

Eileen became such good friends despite the language barrier between the two. It was remarkable.

Back to the Emergency Room, they accessed her port-o-cath, all while Eileen was just exhausted and complained about leg pain in the morning. Of course, this terrified me as the first thing that popped in my head was, she had relapsed. Leg pain was a huge symptom. The team drew blood and did a chest X-ray and started Eileen on Antibiotics right away. Blood work and X-ray came back usual, thank goodness. The other tests that were run took twenty-four to forty-eight hours to come back. The doctor wanted us to be admitted to watch Eileen for at least forty-eight hours. We finally got up to our room around 2:00 p.m.; I went and grabbed lunch for us, and Leeny was back to acting like her usual self. We ate and started watching a movie. Pat was with us. We all fell asleep and woke up to a nurse coming in to take Leeny's vitals. The nurse was concerned with her diagnostic number, which was twenty-five, so she retook it; when it returned the same, she called in another nurse who then decided they would check her vitals every fifteen minutes. They just hooked the cuff to her arm, and the machine took her blood pressure every fifteen minutes, as they discussed. They looked concerned, which made me concerned, worried, and confused. We didn't understand what was happening or why.

Meanwhile, Eileen was still fast asleep. She slept for three hours, and every once in a while, she would start sweating again. The team would check her pulse and fingertips to make sure they were expected. The head doctor came in with all the nurses, and she wanted to wake Eileen up to see if it would change her blood pressure readings. We struggled to wake Leeny as she fought us on wanting to sleep. Her numbers went to a more acceptable, standard number, thankfully, but they still decided to start extra saline 300cc in one hour, which was a lot.

April 1, 1999

We are at the clinic for a push of vincristine and two weeks of prednisone. Eileen will get another injection of vincristine next week. This is the first time since Eileen's diagnosis that she has gotten an IV, what we call a "doggy board" I am so nervous and scared for her because I know she is terrified. I ask Heavenly Father for strength for both her and myself.

Eileen had her port taken out on the tenth of March, and she had it for approximately seven months. We asked the doctors if we could keep it; Leeny is so proud of her port-a-cath, she even shows everyone. She took it to school with her to show to her classmates. The day before surgery, Eileen learned how to ride her bike without training wheels. She was so excited in the PACU (recovery room) that she told me she wanted to ride her bike when we got home when she woke up.

I remember Eileen cried uncontrollably when she woke up. She told me she was all alone and that I was not in the room with her. She cried more and told me the nurses put a mask over her face. I was heartbroken in tears; I explained that I could not be in the room but that Heavenly Father was there with her. She looked up at me with her sweet big brown eyes, and she looked at me, barely awake, "Grandma Eileen was there." Grandma Eileen was Pat, Eileen's Dad's, mother who had passed away from breast cancer years ago. My body was covered in goosebumps. I genuinely believe that Grandma Eileen was there with my Leeny, watching over her.

May 3, 1999

Today we had to get blood counts checked; Eileen had her finger pricked, which she hated. Eileen did not even cry today. She said it hurt a little. She is getting so used to this whole life of hers. I know that this experience had just made Eileen such a strong, loving, and caring child. She looks at the new children in the clinic at times, and I can see the sadness in her eyes. She notices the other children's hair thinning out, and she looks up at me and tells me to "look at that poor baby or little kid." She tells me she hopes they get better, and I tell her we will pray for all the sick children. I always pray that our visits to the clinic will get easier for Eileen and me. But it just brings everything to reality and the whole illness, and it is very depressing at times.

CHAPTER TWO

White Water Rapids

On June 4th, 1998, I was diagnosed with Acute Lymphoblastic Leukemia at nearly five years old. Leukemia is the most common type of childhood cancer, with the best prognosis, easiest to treat, and longest to treat.

I was treated at Texas Children's Hospital in Houston. That is where I underwent two and a half years of treatment which consisted of chemotherapy, vincristine, and methotrexate. Chemotherapy treatments were used to kill the cancer cells in my body. There were three stages of treatment. Number one—Induction lasted twenty-eight days, and its goal was to "induce" a remission; hopefully, at the end of the twenty-eight days, we would not be able to find evidence of Leukemia in my bone marrow. Next, vincristine (VCR) was given to me once a week for four doses given by IV push. The side effects were almost all reversible when I was done with the drug. The side effects consisted of jaw pain, constipation, abdominal pain, tingling or numbness in my fingers and toes, and hair loss. Number two—consolidation (six months) and maintenance (two years).

People often ask me if I remember treatment since I was so young. The answer is yes, I remember. Most memories became repressed; however, over the years, and as I started to write my story, memories began flooding back to me.

My earliest memory is when I had to have the procedure to put in my port-o-cath. This is a device used to draw blood and give treatments. It is placed under the skin and was placed on the right side of my chest. A port-o-cath is attached to a catheter that is guided into a large vein above the right side of my heart. I remember being in a very bright hallway where I was separated from my parents and then taken into a very bright large room where I was then placed on a bed, then the nurses put a mask over my face, and I was knocked out.

Another memory was while eating dinner with my family when we lived in Kingwood in the beginning stages of my treatment. I remember my hair starting to fall out and onto my dinner plate. After dinner, my mom told me we had to shave my head. I was devastated, but it was something that was inevitable. My brothers and dad also shaved their heads in support, which made it not so bad after all. After our head shaving party, I remember having to get in the bathtub to get all the shaved hair off my neck. I loved my bubble baths, so it made it all a little better.

I remember the hospital constantly feeling so grey. It always felt gloomy. But luckily, I always had my mom with me, so it wasn't so bad. Mama made my hospital days more like a trip through the wardrobe into Narnia. She turned my pole that carried my medication into what we called a "beanie pole," covered in my collection of beanie babies. She'd let me stand on the pole while she pushed me up and down the hallways. We became friends with a child my age, Luis, who had just had his leg amputated from a cancerous tumor. My mom and Luis' brother would put on wagon races. We'd sit in our wagons while they would push us and our beanie poles full throttle through the halls. Looking back on it, that was kind of dangerous and could have gone south really quickly, but at the time, those were the best days.

L-Asparaginase (ASP) was a shot that was given to me in my thigh twice a week for a total of six doses. What was different about this shot was that my mom was the one who distributed it to me. We would be at home, and she could give it to me without us having to go into the clinic. Can you imagine being a mother and having to go through training to give your baby girl weekly shots? I cannot begin to understand what my sweet parents had to endure and what they sacrificed in the fight for my life. I will never forget that almost every time I would receive these shots, I would sit on the lap of either my dad or a grandparent. They did this to comfort my mom and me. The consistent support I had was something some people did not have, and for that, I will always be thankful.

My least favorite days were when I received a spinal tap. This procedure was used to treat the brain to prevent leukemia from spreading to my brain. The three drugs used were methotrexate, ARA-C, and hydrocortisone. The many terrible side effects included headaches, fever, nausea, and vomiting. My parents would have to wake me up super early, and I wasn't allowed to eat or drink any fluids. Then, we would have to wait for what felt like forever to be called back into the treatment room. Being that young and waiting that long on an empty stomach wasn't an easy task. When they would call my name, I would immediately start crying because I knew what that meant. It meant I had to leave my mom. The nurses would have to pry me from her, and I would get taken back to the big white room. I would lie in the hospital bed and cry while I watched the syringe filled with what looked like milk travel into my IV and make me fall asleep. When I would finally wake up, I always had my mom or dad, sometimes both, there to greet me. They always had my "T.T." blanket and my teddy bear ready for me. Afterward, we would walk down this long hallway towards the elevator and stop to get a snack at the "candy cart." Lays sour cream and onion chips and Sprite were my "go-to" choices.

Prednisone was a medication used in my treatment. It was a steroid given three times a day for twenty-eight days, given by mouth via liquid or pill. The side effects of the prednisone were high blood pressure, an increase of appetite, mood swings, high blood sugar, weight gain, upset stomach, and trouble sleeping. It was the most horrible medicine I have ever had to put in my mouth. My mom had an ingenious idea to help me swallow pills by using mini M&M's—this was just the trick I needed to manage my medications. However, the prednisone was a beast of its own. That pill would touch my tongue and leave a lasting taste in my mouth; that's something I can't even begin to describe other than disgusting. My mom would try to mix it in yogurt, food, anything, just to get me to take it, but like a dog, I could smell that junk from a mile away. I even started saying, "you try it," and I got multiple people to try it like fools. They all made the same face of utter disgust. Eventually, we found some aid in helping me get this particular medicine in my body. Pickles. Yes, pickles. As soon as I would swallow the prednisone, I would chase it down with pickles of any shape, size, and cut. This medication not only was nasty for me to take, but it also made me blow up like a balloon. I went from being a cute, petite little girl to a little bald chunk. Looking back at the pictures makes me laugh, but I have to admit, I was still cute.

CHAPTER THREE

Wavelength

Being able to call someone your "friend" means you trust this person, you feel supported by this person, and there is a bond between you and that person. Friendships have played a vital role in my life. Friendships are made up of the people we choose to have in our lives. With family, we have no choice, and God blesses us with those people we share blood with. Friendships are up to us! I have had many friends throughout my life, some for a short period and some lasting relationships I still carry on to this day and will for the rest of my life.

The right kind of friendships—healthy friendships, if you will—can at times bring more happiness into our lives than anything else in the world. Nothing can compare to the way friendships impact your life. The sense of belonging you receive, and the ability to mentally lift one another up in dark times, are truly remarkable. The word "friend" has always meant something special to me. It is something remarkable to be a positive light in another person's life and to create a support system that helps you to navigate through the crazy waves of life.

Jazmin B. is my earliest memory of a friend. For years, her mother, Shan, was my mom's best friend, so it was predetermined that we would become best friends before birth. Jazmin was just that, my best friend. At four years old, we were inseparable—always playing every chance we could, eating Taco Bueno, watching movies. We were just the sweetest of friends. We both sucked our thumbs and had what we called a "T.T." blanket that we would carry around everywhere we went.

When I got sick with cancer, I remember being bald and the feelings I would feel when people would look at me with sad eyes. However, the first time Jazmin saw me without hair, she did not look at me with sad eyes, but more of "oh my gosh, what happened to your hair?!" eyes. That's why she was and will always be considered one of my best friends. Jazmin did not look at me and see a cancer patient. She saw me for me in the purest of ways; she treated me no differently than before my diagnosis.

Being a part of the cancer community meant making friends with other current cancer patients—children. Children the same age as me, younger and some older. I met some kids on clinic days, just waiting to go back for our checkups and some during treatment stays.

My second round of treatment, which consisted of starting with a spinal tap (my least favorite) to protect my central nervous system, was then followed by a seventy-two-hour treatment of chemotherapy. I recall being in my room with the door open, my mom sitting on the chair next to me, and I began to hear a baby crying. I listened to the same cry throughout the day. My mom went next door to check on the baby and met a nurse by the doorway who was looking after her. My mom spoke with the nurse and came back to tell me it was a beautiful baby girl next door. A sweet, beautiful baby was being treated for cancer. Can you believe that? Looking back, it's hard to fathom little four-year-old me fighting for my life but a baby fighting off cancer? How is that fair? The shock and anger that filled my soul with not having the ability to understand why God would do this to such a sweet baby was indescribable. At four, that's how I felt. Instead of worrying about friends, toys, and starting preschool, I constantly thought about baby Jazmin and wished I could take her cancer on myself and have her be free of the disease.

The door to baby Jazmin's room was always open, and her cries filled the hospital floor. Even when she was not crying, I could hear her cry. Her door was always empty because no one was there with her; only the nurses cared for her. I do not know where her parents were throughout the day and night, and that was hard for me to understand. My mom was always with me, and when she was not, my dad was. I always had someone there to hold my hand, my puke bucket—someone was always there to support me every step of the way. I was fortunate. I was blessed in that aspect. Baby Jazmin's mom would occasionally come in the evenings for no more than an hour each time. I am unsure of where she spent the rest of her day, maybe at work, maybe taking care of other kids? All I know is those nurses cared for and loved that sweet baby. My mom would often stand in the doorway of baby Jazmin's room and just be there. That was my mama. I know I am sharing the aspect of my life and treatment, but I can only imagine what my mom and dad went through.

Jazmin cried day in and day out, day after day. It was rare for her not to be crying. Maybe that's why, as I have grown older, it causes me a significant amount of anxiety to hear a baby crying. Isn't it strange how something that happened over fourteen years ago is something I am still dealing with today? That's how trauma works, though, right? The memories I carry with me cause this unbearable pain in situations that a person who did not have my background would consider normal and would deal with it accordingly. But for me, I have to make the crying stop before my body and mind end up back in my four-year-old body and that hospital room with memories like a tsunami rushing through my being.

One day I woke up to silence—not one cry was uttered from Jazmin's room. There was a calm feeling of peace in finding silence. The crying finally stopped. Why? I remember asking my mom, "Did baby Jazmin get to go home?" My mom went into the hallway and came back to my room. She looked sad, but she smiled at me. I do not remember her giving me an answer, but that gave me the answer I dreaded. I was only four years old and had to comprehend that a baby had just died! This was not only unfair to me, but unexplainable. All I could do was pray and hope God needed that baby as an angel. I never asked my mom questions; I saw her sad eyes and left them at that.

Corina was someone I met in the hospital during treatment as well. I was from the United States, Corina was from Mexico. I spoke English, and she spoke Spanish. Corina's family left their home in Mexico to come to Houston, Texas. Her family left everything and everyone they knew to fight for their daughter's life. Houston's medical center is one of the best in the United States. Corina's family wanted to give her the best shot at a life they could. And they did just that.

Her mom and my mom grew close and bonded as mothers of pediatric cancer patients. Corina did not speak English; she only spoke Spanish. I only spoke English and didn't know a lick of Spanish despite being a quarter Hispanic and having a mom, plus all of her family being Spanish speakers! Can you believe that? My mom never taught us Spanish! To my sweet Mama's defense, I do not know if I or any of my three brothers would have listened or been good students for her.

Back to my friendship with Corina, we became closer and closer as we spent more time together despite our language barriers. I remember when Corina had her bone marrow transplant and missed her dearly as we couldn't see one another. A bone marrow transplant is a procedure performed to replace damaged bone marrow, transplanting blood stem cells that travel to the bone marrow where they produce new blood cells and promote the healthy growth of new marrow.

You see, when you have to go through a bone marrow transplant, you spend ten days in isolation before your transplant. You then spend several days in isolation after your transplant. So bone marrow transplant patients are under rigorous isolation procedures after receiving transplants. This is to protect the patient from contact with germs or infections.

I do remember being able to play while looking at one another through a clear glass window. Without talking, being next to each other without any barriers, we simply played with one another. We would smile, laugh, and in those moments, we were just kids being kids—not kids fighting for our lives. The unique part about my friendship with Corina was that we connected as children despite our differences.

Cancer is not something that cares what color your skin is, your gender, your age—cancer is not prejudiced against anyone or anything. Cancer lies; cancer cheats. Cancer is one fight that is not always a fair battle. In the end, as a patient, all you can do is fight your fight-pray and hope for an outcome in your favor.

CHAPTER FOUR

Hurricane Season

I went to a camp known as Camp Periwinkle in Texas, which the Periwinkle Foundation hosted. This camp was named after the plant that is used in the chemotherapy agent vincristine. Camp Periwinkle was founded in 1983 by Dr. Paul Gerson in hopes of providing children being treated at Texas Children's Hospital an opportunity to "just feel normal" for one week. This camp was a camp for cancer patients, survivors, and siblings from Texas Children's Hospital. This was an excellent opportunity for kids to just be kids, meet children fighting the same fight as one another, and meet survivors to look up to in admiration.

This camp was the best, from the fantastic staff of counselors to all the activities and entertainment they provided. Camp Periwinkle was located on a massive amount of acreage, where we were split into cabins, each with a theme and name. We had daily schedules that were filled with endless activities. They offered canoeing, fishing, horseback riding, rock climbing, archery, bike riding, and water sports. The camp also put on an Olympic day where everyone was divided into two teams, and we competed against one another for the champion title. This camp was something magical for me, and I'm sure for everyone who ever attended. For the weeks I was able to be a camper, I was able to feel like a normal kid, not the kid with cancer. We were all kids who had or were fighting cancer which made us all equal. I met some fantastic people during those impactful years I attended; two that stand out, in particular, were Allison and Taylor.

There was a "downside" to camp. It was at Camp Periwinkle where I first heard the term "terminal." This word was used in reference to one of my cabin mates, Tayler, who was only a teenager and was suffering from several cancerous tumors throughout her body. Having "terminal" cancer means there is nothing left for the doctors to do, no more treatments that will work, and that heaven is on the horizon. When I returned home from camp, I waited quite a while before giving this camper a call. Her mother would answer every time and let me know she was too tired for a phone call. Finally, the last time I called, her mom answered and informed me her daughter had gone to be with the Lord. I froze upon hearing this devastating news, sunk into a ball, and began to cry before I hung up the phone.

Taylors' obituary read, *"Tayler, sixteen, passed quietly on October 2, 2006, at her home after a long battle with cancer." Sixteen years of life, with so much more life to offer and give, taken away just like that. This was someone's daughter, someone's sister, someone's granddaughter. This was a young girl who loved going to school, being outdoors, art, and just living life.*

This was my first personal experience with death, and I had barely made it to the sixth grade! Grasping the concept of a child dying of a disease that I had overcome is a weight that I can only describe as unbearable. During the following weeks, I slowly sunk into what I now know as depression, guilt-ridden from being a survivor. I was ashamed of being alive while this young girl had already left this world. My heart broke for her family, who I had never even met. But I didn't need to know them to feel the deep empathy that overwhelmed every ounce of my being.

After Tayler passed away, I searched for her on social media, on a website called Myspace. I had found her page. "Life is a Highway" by Rascal Flatts was the song featured on her page and played as I looked through her pictures and posts. I smiled as I listened to the words because life is precisely that—a highway. So many different roads go in different directions, loops, and turns. Every road will lead you to a different door that will shape the course of your life forever. At the top of Tayler's page read, "Dare to be Different." Those four words have taken on a new meaning as I have gotten older. But I haven't forgotten that quote. It is okay to be different, it is okay to think differently, it is okay to look different, and it is okay to go through life differently than others. And with that, I will always dare to be different and only pray those differences will one day be able to help someone else.

Chapter Five

Eye of the Storm

That same year, in 2006, my dad came home from work one day to inform my family that a boy who lived down the street from us had been diagnosed with the same cancer I had when I was little—leukemia. The day he was released from the Texas Children's Hospital, my mom and I walked down to his family home. I packed a few items from my treatment that I had at home to share. When I walked in, I quickly realized who he was. Nick was a year older than me and happened to ride the same bus I took to school. He was also one of the boys who were always loud and obnoxious on this bus. Looking back on that, it's pretty funny, but I was not amused at the time.

When I first met Nick, I explained what would happen and how he would feel after chemotherapy and treatment in general. He did not ask any questions; why? Because Nick was a fighter through and through. One of the things we had in common was our love of soccer. Nick lived and breathed soccer. He might have always been the smallest on the field, but that boy was determined and mighty. As months went by, our friendship quickly grew. We had an indescribable bond that only would have sparked through his cancer diagnosis. We would go on bike rides to get TCBY frozen yogurt, we would battle it out on Guitar Hero, and sometimes I would have

20

to plug my ears as Nick would be screaming at strangers he would be playing with on XBOX. He was very serious with his gaming.

Our favorite outing was attending every Houston Dynamo soccer game. In 2006, the Dynamo were new to the MLS and played out of Robertson Stadium at the University of Houston. Boy, did Nick love his boys in orange. Nick's doctor introduced him to a local sports commentator, Glenn Davis, who has his own radio show in Houston called "Soccer Matters". Glenn loved Nick, and Nick adored Glenn. Nick was soon introduced to Stuart Holden, Mike Chabala, and Craig Waibel, some of the top players who played with the Houston Dynamo. These guys were amazing to my dear friend. They would swing by his house, stop in during treatment days, and always made sure Nick had tickets to games he felt well enough to attend.

I'll never forget a game we all attended, and Nick was sitting between my dad and me. Dad was chowing down on some salted peanuts, and Nick was getting aggravated and annoyed as he could not eat peanuts at the time, I think because of the salt. Nick gave my dad the dirtiest look. My dad tried to assure Nick the peanuts were not any good, and Nick fired back, "Oh yeah right, Mr. Dowd. You sound like a cow eating those peanuts". My dad and I could not stop laughing.

The year Nick and I both dove into the high school dating scene was a memorable one for sure. As for Nick and me, we both loved each other dearly, looked out for one another, and innocently cared for one another. So, when it came to dating other people, we were naturally protective. Why didn't we ever date? I'm not sure. There were times when Nick would reach for my hand or slightly touch his fingers to mine in the car, and sometimes, I would leave my hand touching his, and sometimes I would pull it away. I think perhaps I knew deep down what was coming even when the end was years away. I was protecting myself and my heart in ways I shouldn't have had to at that age.

So back to dating. Nick started dating a girl in my grade in middle school. I was in seventh grade, and he was in eighth. It was a typical middle school relationship, walking one another to classes, meeting at lockers, and sitting next to each other in the lunchroom. Why was this annoying to me? Because honestly, I did not think anyone was good enough or deserved Nick. And at the end of the day, who else was taking care of him the way I did, other than his family? Not that girl, I can tell you that much not long after sitting with Nick in his living room. He got a phone call from someone (not his current girlfriend). I could not hear what was said clearly, but Nick got off the phone and looked upset. Of course, I asked what happened, and he let me know that the girl he was dating broke things off with him. The sad part was that his now ex-girlfriend didn't dare to break up with him herself. She had a friend do it for her as she sat next to her on the other end of the phone. Now I understand not wanting to hurt someone's feelings but seriously have some respect. If I remember correctly, I had some profound words with those two girls, and I don't think I ever let Nick know that.

One day Nick came to me upset, he was on the golf team at school, and two boys who played golf were giving him a hard time. Now, if I had been made aware of this sooner, I would have taken care of it. I overheard these two particular boys making fun of Nick because he was so small, and the backpack he wore was bigger than his body. I will give them that; his bag was huge and always filled with his books; I am honestly not sure if he used his locker to each their own. Anyway, I had words with those nasty boys. I absolutely laid into them with my words. I believe I said something along the lines of "How dare you to mess with Nick when you know good and damn well what he is fighting. He's fighting for his life, while you two are healthy as an ox and have the audacity to tease this kid over his backpack"? I used much harsher words, was firm and direct with the point I was trying to make. In tears, they apologized to me, and the following week Nick let me know those boys went to his house and formally apologized. My work was done.

Naturally, I met someone in high school my freshman year. This new boyfriend of mine was a year older than me in the sophomore class with Nick. He was a goalie on the soccer team, so Nick knew him well. I don't think Nick was thrilled when hearing the news, but he never shared that with me. Our school put on a Sadie Hawkins dance every year where the girls would ask the guys to be their dates to that particular dance. I, of course, asked Nick; I filled his room with balloons while he was in the clinic that day and put a big sign in his room that said "Sadie"? Not to my surprise, Nick was a grump about having so many balloons in his room, but I think he was happy I asked him. We decided to join his class group for dinner, party bus, and after-party. This was about Nick having fun, not me. I wouldn't say I liked dances and dancing, for that matter. The boy I'd been talking to and who would later be someone I dated was in that group as well. Nick danced his little tush off all night long and let me stand in a corner knowing good and darn well I would never be caught dancing, which I very much appreciated.

After the dance, we went to "Pump it Up," an indoor place with bouncy jumpers, slides, and activities. Towards the end of the night, a projector was brought out to watch a movie; everyone found a mat and laid on the floor. Most of the dates were couples, so I paired off and laid on a mat next to the boy I liked. We were far enough from one another but had our hands in the middle, slightly touching, but to where no one would notice. And I swear to you, out of nowhere, Nick came and scooted his body in between the other young man and me and got really comfy before starting to chow down on some popcorn. Oh, did I glare at him while he gave me a big ole grin in return.

As the years went by, Nick's cancer would go into remission and then soon after would return. Over and over. Every time taking a piece of my heart and mental state. I would slip into a depression every time my mom called me downstairs to inform me of Nick's worsening condition. I wouldn't eat, knowing that was one thing I had control over. I wouldn't sleep, and I repressed any and all of my feelings with Nick.

You see, Nick's cancer started in his blood, he relapsed, and his doctors decided he should have a bone marrow transplant. Soon after, cancer then spread to his central nervous system. When it traveled to his central nervous system, his doctors decided to put a new port-a-cath in his head so the treatments would go directly into his central nervous system. I woke up early the day of that procedure and went with Nick and his parents. We all waited in the waiting room anxiously for Nick to come out of his procedure, and he did, with a smile on his face.

After the central nervous system was cancerous, his cancer spread to one of his testicles. His parents were left with an unimaginable decision to remove that testicle. Not long after, cancer spread to the other testicle. It was then I realized Nick was going to be unable to have children in the future. This broke my heart. We were so young, and I knew then I would adopt children with Nick when the time came. Of course, I never told him that, but I knew adoption would be in my future.

During every hospital stay, I would visit. We'd watch movies; one I remember particularly was "Superbad." Nick would crack up at those scenes, which were generally very inappropriate. We watched this movie in his hospital room as one of the raunchier scenes came on, and his nurse walked into the room. I, of course, was mortified; Nick laughed his head off. That was the difference between us—I would overthink what others may be thinking, and Nick just lived; he was always living in the moment. He didn't care.

During treatments, I would always hold his puke bucket and hold his hand when he needed support. I'll never forget Nick looking at me from his hospital bed. The last things he said to me were, "Eileen, you're a great friend, you've been a great friend. I love you, Eileen. You've always been such a good friend to me. I want you to have my car; I'm sorry I didn't get to the rims." If you knew Nick, you'd know how much he loved his blue, two-door Nissan Altima he received on his sixteenth birthday. Those are words I will never forget.

One day I was sitting in Nick's hospital room chair next to his bedside. We were watching TV—well, I was watching TV. Nick was in and out of sleep. His eyes would roll around and not really focus on anything. His lips were chapped, his skin tone was more of a yellow color. His mother was also in the room. We smelled something that resembled feces. Nick's mom lifted his blanket, exposing Nick, who was covered in precisely what we thought. Finally, Nick's eyes opened, and I made sure to keep my eyes locked with his, smiled, and mouthed, "It is okay." The nurses came in and cleaned him up, and I left the room to make sure he had privacy. Nick's nurses and social workers would tell me he would always ask for me whenever I was away. This warmed my heart, knowing he knew when I was and was not present.

Every time I walked onto the cancer floor and down to Nick's room, someone would always greet me. And every time I stopped to talk to whoever was there at the time, that person always had the most affirming words to say regarding my relationship with Nick; I did not realize how incredibly validating the words said to me were. One of Nick's social workers always let me know Nick asked for me. She said any time I was not at the hospital, and he would ask, "Where is Eileen?" It truly warmed my heart knowing Nick knew when I was there and when I was not because honestly, he was so close to death that I did not know half the time if he felt my presence. Then, Nick's uncle Steve came into town and gave me a big hug and said in my ear, "I see a huge part of you in Nick; you will always be a part of this family." It took everything in me not to break down right there. And then there was the sweetest, most sassy woman, Nick's "Nana". She grabbed me, gave me a big squeeze and looked at my eyes, and told me, "Nick loves you so much. You mean everything to him; you have always been such an amazing friend to him, the way you just sit with him for hours even when he was not feeling his best; you are an amazing friend." The words of affirmation and validation from Nick's people, the people that knew him best, those words will permanently be embedded in my heart.

Many of Nick's high school friends, who he'd known since elementary school, would frequently come to me and ask how he was doing. Sometimes I would not know what to tell them, so then I would become angry with them. They, of course, didn't know that because I never expressed it. But at the end of the day, I was the one sitting next to him. I was doing my best to be a support for him while these so-called friends were out doing other things but still dared to come to me for clarification on his condition.

I would be in the hospital room with Nick while he had friends come to visit him. They didn't know what to say to Nick, and they didn't know what to do. They would start crying while sitting next to Nick. I yanked those kids out of that room so fast and told them to get it together and that Nick needed them to show support, not weakness. I explained that they needed to just talk to Nick as if he were engaging in conversation, even though he wasn't capable of doing that.

On November 13, my parents agreed to let me sleep over at the hospital with Nick. I packed my overnight bag and looked forward to being able to spend the time with Nick. When I got to Texas Children's, Nick was fast asleep and resting in his bed. Mrs. Jodie, Nick's mom, was visiting with a family friend. The Houston Dynamo was playing that night, so of course, I had to turn the tv on to watch the game. Mrs. Jodie and I watched the game together over dinner. If I remember correctly, it was a Chipotle night. After the game ended, I began to doze off, and I slept for a few hours before I woke up in an anxious sweat hearing the screams and cries from a baby in the room next door. My mind went back to twelve years prior and hearing baby Jazmin's cries. Is it not crazy how our body and mind react to memories? It took me a minute to realize where I was and remember I was not sick anymore, only to come to the realization of why I was back in that hospital, and that broke my heart just as much. I will never forget that morning I ran into one of my nurses from when I was in treatment, and we caught up for a few minutes when I decided to ask her, "How much longer does Nick have?" She looked at me hesitantly and gave me an answer— three to four days. I choked on my thoughts and words. Three to four days! How could it end like this?

Our school put on a prayer circle in the parking lot before the first period in the last week of Nick's life. Hand in hand, about twenty of Nick's friends prayed one after another. While we were listening to one another's prayers, I kept my head down but in a position where I could see everyone. You could see tears starting to hit the pavement and form circles. I did not want to participate in this particular event as I was already emotionally and mentally drained, but I knew people needed me, and I was looked at as a source of comfort.

So, my turn came, both people beside me squeezed my hands, and I began to pray. "Dear Heavenly Father, I want to thank you for allowing us all to be a part of Nick's life. I ask you now to please free him from any pain or discomfort. Open your arms to him and allow him to live cancer-free in your kingdom." While everyone else prayed for a miracle, I begged for mercy. As I spoke, all I could hear were sniffles and sobs; when I looked up, every person's teardrop puddles tripled in size. The difference between those kids and myself was that I knew exactly what Nick was living through. I knew what he was fighting, and with that knowledge, I also knew the "right thing" for him. The right thing, the merciful thing, was to ask God to open his gates to my dear friend and allow him to live free of this unforgiving disease we call cancer.

On November 16, 2009, my mom and I visited Nick in the hospital as he was slowly deteriorating. He was in and out of consciousness. Before I left, I asked his family and my mom to leave the room to have some privacy. I sat next to his bedside, holding his hand, and told him it was okay. That everything was going to be okay. I told him what a fighter he was and how much I loved him. I asked him to watch over me, no matter where I was, and to know that he better be ready to start a life together when I get to heaven one day. I squeezed his hand and bent over the top of him and kissed his cheek. He very gently squeezed my hand back, and I knew he was listening.

On November 17, 2009, I didn't go to school. I was so anxiety-ridden, depressed, and mentally exhausted. I couldn't get out of bed. My mom came into my room to ask if I wanted to go up to the hospital to see Nick, and at first, I said no. In my mind, I said my goodbyes and couldn't bear to do it again. After a few minutes, I changed my mind and agreed. We stopped to pick up

Nick's grandparents on the way, which took longer than expected. What felt like forever was a forty-minute drive down to the medical center.

We arrived on the cancer floor at 10:30 a.m. We turned the corner from the elevator, and all I could see was a woman crying who then looked up at me and shook her head. I knew what that meant. My mom immediately tried to hug me, and I just could not. I pushed her off of me and did not shed a tear. I walked over and sat in a rocking chair in the hallway and just rocked back and forth.

Nick went to be with the Lord at 10:15 a.m. Fifteen minutes! If only I had been ready earlier, if only picking up Nick's grandparents took less time, I might have been able to see Nick one more time, talk to him one last time. Being fifteen minutes late and missing that opportunity changed me. I, to this day, refuse to be late to anything. And when or if I am late, I am consumed with anxiety.

Nick's social worker, Mithal, came to me and Nick's sister, Dayna. She asked us to follow her into a room to talk. I did not want to speak, but I followed for Dayna's sake. Dayna was two years younger than me and was like a sister to me, and she needed my support. Mithal sat and explained to us what was to come now, the grieving process, and asked us if we had any questions. I knew the routine. Dayna so innocently asked, "So are we going to take Nick home so that he can see the house one more time"? I could not help but let out a little laugh; Dayna laughed too. She was so young, so innocent, and so full of life. She still, to this day, is so full of life. Nick's other social worker asked me if I wanted to see Nick; I was hesitant but said yes. I walked into Nick's room for the last time, and I saw his lifeless, grey-colored body lying in his bed. I walked closer until I was back by his bedside, and I reached for his hand as I always did. He was freezing cold. Cold and stone hard. I will never forget that moment. I looked up and saw Nick's family around him just crying. The hurt, the devastation. I just wished I could take it all away. Next, we took Nick's hand and made clay molds of them. Nick's family was able to take those home and keep them—that was something special.

The days that followed were a blur. After missing so much school, I had to return to my classes the day after Nick passed away. How was that enough time for me to deal with my emotions? To put it plainly, it was not and would never be enough time. Everyone stared at me as I walked through the halls of the school, as I walked from class to class. I could not walk through the hallway with my head up anymore; it felt like everyone was looking at me differently, with their sad eyes. This made me both sad and angry.

Why did I lose my best friend? Why, after everything I had been through up to that point, did I have to experience such a loss? How could I make sense of this? I could not. I remember leaving one of my classes and walking through the halls entirely and utterly drained. I locked eyes with my friend Kassie's sister, Kacie. We walked towards one another, and she grabbed me before I turned the corner, and I just fell into her arms, and she held me while stroking my hair as I began to sob, and she began to cry herself. That hug meant so much to me, and I don't think that's something I ever let her know. That's all I needed was to allow myself to feel comforted by someone. It is not like my parents didn't try because they did. I just wouldn't let it happen. I guess that was the time my mental struggles began to take hold of me mindfully, and I quite plainly wanted to protect them from the darkness that was taking hold of my mind.

Through high school, I had a teacher who also coached me in soccer, Mr. Filson. He opened his doors to me whenever I needed. I could go into his classroom in the middle of my day and just lie behind his desk and cry while he taught his classes. He sat with me while I cried; he let me stay in his room during lunch hours and made sure I always had something to eat in my belly. At that point, I was five foot four and weighing about 115 pounds, definitely not a healthy look. But again, food was my only form of control at that time.

I sat in Mr. Filson's room during lunch every day for months. You see, when I returned to school and walked into the cafeteria with some of my friends, I turned my head and saw a big yellow banner in the middle of the lunchroom that read "Livestrong." This was in honor of Nick. I cannot begin to express how badly I wanted to run up to that sign and rip it off the wall. I was so angry and filled with sadness. Rather than acting on those emotions, I got up and went to Mr. Filson's classroom for what felt like a sanctuary from all the madness.

People were taking turns going up to the sign and signing it with notes of love and remembrance. So why did this fill my entire being with rage? I saw people who didn't even know Nick, people he didn't even like (not that they knew) signing this banner. People were crying, holding one another, and writing on this poster. And this was something I just couldn't stand. Where were they during clinic days? During procedures? When he was on his deathbed? Looking back, this was highly unfair of me; Nick's death rocked a lot of lives. Regardless of his relationships with these classmates, everyone was grieving. But in turn, I saw the strength I displayed in being there for my friend, Nick.

The day after Nick passed away, I walked into my "Teen Leadership" classroom. This class was actually my favorite class; we learned life skills and had weekly subjects on which we would have to write speeches and read aloud to our classmates and teacher. This class was probably the most therapeutic class I could have been in at the time. On the day of our speeches, my classmates and I were each given three "affirmation" cards where we would write affirmations to three speakers of our choice. This was a time to tell one another what we thought of their shared stories, validate feelings and just connect with one another. I realize now how much I needed those things and that class during this time in my life.

Back on November 18, 2009, I walked into my classroom, and all of my classmates looked at me as I walked in, and all I could see were the sad eyes and expressions on their faces. See, I had shared speeches about my battle with cancer as a child and many stories of my friendship with Nick, so they knew the devastation I was feeling very well. It was my day to read my speech which happened to be about someone who had made a difference in my life. My person was Nick. I went up to my teacher and asked if I could skip this exercise given the circumstances. She looked at me, smiled, and told me speaking about Nick would be good for me. At the time, I disagreed, but now looking back, I see I showed strength at that moment to all my classmates. I stood in front of my classmates, and I began to speak. As tears began to well up in my eyes, my throat choked up with every other word I was about to say. I began to speak—all I wanted to do was burst into tears. I shared my love for Nick, the type of friendship we had, and the difference he had made by being in my life. I kept my head down for the duration of my speech, but when I lifted my head as I finished, everyone, boys, girls, and my teacher, all had tears either falling down their cheeks or tears fighting their way out. I touched everyone in that room by displaying strength and perseverance. I wanted everyone around me to think I was stronger than I was at the time, and I did it well. When I reached for my affirmation bag at the end of the class period, my bag was filled; I had a note from every person in the class offering comfort, validation, and thanks. My teacher, Mrs. F, wrote to me, *"Eileen, you have already accomplished so much in your life through your battle with cancer and your pain surrounding your relationship with Nick. Thank you for making us all laugh with your wonderful sense of humor. We felt your loss after we lost Nick, and it was humbling to us all. Leaders are always in the spotlight, and others are watching how you handle the rough spots in your lives. You have been a wonderful example of the attitude I hope all my students will eventually achieve, which is one of hope and wonder. You gave us all hope with your story about your battle with Leukemia. You make us all wonder about our futures and what life will be like in five to ten years. Regardless of the struggles you will face, I know you will be happy and have very strong relationships because that is what you have shown us is important in life. You are a treasure."* To this day, I have kept that note.

* * * * *

When it came time for Nick's funeral, Nick's parents asked if I would walk in with them and sit in the front row with all of their family. I was honored. I walked into the family room and met Nick's mother with a hug and told her I was going to marry her son. She smiled. The doors opened to the chapel, and I had never seen a room so full. This was a large area, and every single seat was filled as people were shoulder to shoulder with one another.

I made my way to the front row, and when I looked up, I spotted a blue urn. I tried so hard to fight back the tears that were trying so hard to pour out of my eyes. My friend, my beautiful friend, was in that urn; all that was left of him were his ashes. I listened to Glenn Davis give Nick's eulogy. It was so well written I feel the need to share.

* * * * *

"Nick Doize touched and stirred my heart, taught me about courage, bravery, dignity, and grace under the toughest of circumstances. Today we celebrate and honor Nick and his life, a life that has been so enriching to so many and has touched us all in different ways. There are not enough words to describe how unique Nick was. To me, Nick is a true hero, a study of living. He faced for what most people, is unfaceable. Nick was an example of one who took all there was out of life. I was fortunate enough to have an email exchange with Dr. Pat Thompson at Texas Children's Hospital years ago which led to my friendship with Nick, his father Jeff, his mother Jodie, and his sister Dayna who I have stood in awe watching so gracefully love and care for their beautiful son and brother. I am simply amazed at how many lives Nick has touched, how many connections he has made, how many friends he has, and how many people he has brought together. In a world of hype, celebrities, and toys, Nick reminded us vividly of what is important…love, family, friends, and a passion for living. Many know of Nick, and his courage and passion for life yet were never fortunate enough to have met him. Ask most soccer fans about Nick Doize…. And they would know him. He was equally adept socially with his peers and adults. He had an uncanny ability to read other people… I marveled at how he could seamlessly relate to anyone, despite all the challenges he was going through. He was a beautiful magnet with a smile that would bring you to your knees. I loved the wonderment and excitement in his eyes. I knew that I was

fortunate to have crossed paths with Nick. Nick and I shared a passion called soccer. We spoke of one-day being partners calling soccer games on TV… I told him, "Nick, you will make a fantastic analyst because you have beautiful opinions and insights." We did this on several occasions while watching games at my house. We critiqued, we praised, and we analyzed soccer matches. He was brilliant and knowledgeable about the sport, and he did have great opinions. In fact, he was not afraid to even criticize me. I called him my personal executive producer/agent. Mostly we laughed and smiled. One day Nick came on the radio show with me in a sports bar setting to talk about his charity at the time and an upcoming soccer tournament he was hosting. For those that were there, it was an amazing moment. Of course, Nick was not daunted about going on the radio and speaking to a room of adults. Nick came on the radio with no fear and described the tournament beautifully without skipping a beat. This was easy for him. I later told him and others that I was fifteen years into the radio and television business, and I was hoping to one day be as smooth as he was. Nick had a comedic side, and his trading of barbs with Dynamo professional soccer players like Craig Waibel and Stuart Holden, players he so loved, are legendary. One of his favorite targets of jokes was his doctor, Dr. Pat Thompson, at Texas Children's. On one trip, Nick's family made it to Seattle, and I was fortunate to be included with Nick and his Dad, Jeff. We were in a beautiful setting on the water at Lake Union in the Pacific Northwest. We were bathing in the sunshine. We were living it up, eating Dungeness crab and some of the finest seafood, watching seaplanes land, birds and boats pass by while lounging totally relaxed. We got an idea to call Dr. Thompson and rub it in a little bit. Nick apologized jokingly for eating Dungeness crab, being on the water, and vacationing, as we called it, living large! That day, at that moment, Nick was teaching me to live largely. Nick knew what was really important in life. What he knew was true of life, that people should have passion. Anytime I drive by a soccer field, I think of Nick. You have heard this before . . . life is not measured by the number of breaths that we take but the moments that take our breath away. Nick took our breath away; he was authentic and the real deal. I don't know if I will ever have the good fortune of having a son in life, but if I ever do, I hope he is just like Nick."

* * * * *

Glenn Davis did my friend Nick justice in that eulogy. Afterward, I listened to countless people share stories that told what a difference Nick had made in their lives—family, teachers, friends, soccer teammates, and professional soccer players. Nick's life here on earth was short. But the impact he left on people's hearts will be with all of us forever. Everyone learned how precious every life moment is and not to take a single bit of it for granted.

Losing someone like Nick, who meant the world to me, is something I wouldn't wish upon my worst enemy. It was a loss that shocked me to my core. The grief I was feeling made the world feel dark and gloomy. I stopped seeing the colors and joys of life. My world had been tainted with loss. And I didn't know how to properly communicate that to anyone. It is not that the people around me would not check on me or try to console me, but I frankly would not let anyone close to me or open up about how I was feeling. I did not want anyone to know the dark thoughts that consumed me—how could anyone possibly help clear those from my mind? I didn't want to become a burden for anyone else, so I closed myself off from the world instead of thinking I could work through it on my own; I was wrong, so very wrong.

My dad left me an eight-page note about two weeks before Nick's passing, and one passage read, "Let Nick's life be an example to you, appreciate every moment that you are given. Be happy, upbeat, and be a positive influence on those around you. Never forget Nick or his fighting spirit! Continue to support and promote activities that will assist those that are suffering. Every day there is someone like Nick who is beginning their journey through childhood cancer. Life is all about knowledge and experiences. Be an instrument of good. Nick would want you to be happy and committed to accomplishing your goals. Never quit—and appreciate the life you have been given." It might have taken me a decade to act on that passage, but every road I took in life led me up to this point, writing about traumas healthily, and I can honestly say I am now living a life my sweet Nick would be more than proud of.

CHAPTER SIX

Murky Waters

A friendship I was more than blessed with is that friendship I share with Kassie. Kassie is someone who came into my life at the most pivotal point in my life, during my most trying of times. Kassie was kind enough to share some of her memories of our friendship, my struggles, and what she has learned from it all.

* * * * *

Looking back on my life, I find it so interesting the people I have come in contact with at certain times in my life. Without realizing it at the time, these people may have needed me, or I may have needed them without thinking twice about it. The placement of people in our lives is no coincidence. People come into our lives at specific times with and for a purpose; there is usually a more significant meaning behind it. At least, I think so. One person that came into my life that needed me more than I would know, Eileen Dowd.

It was not until my sophomore year of high school where I met Eileen. I knew of her from mutual friends but had not had the opportunity to really get to know her until that year. I remember that time frame because it was around the same time as Homecoming in the fall of 2009. All I knew of Eileen was a fantastic soccer player. She loved supporting the Houston Dynamo by wearing her orange gear. Lastly, she always sported her yellow "Livestrong" bracelet.

As I said, I believe we are placed in people's lives at specific times for a reason. Meeting Eileen and becoming close friends was no coincidence. Right when Eileen and I became friends, Nick was extremely sick and bedridden in the hospital. My memories of those months are something I can only describe as "dark." Everything about it, Nick being sick, Eileen had to go through something like watching her best friend slowly die at such a young age. Dark. For me, looking back on it, I was watching someone I loved and cared about dealing with something that most people will not ever have to deal with in the entirety of their life. For me, this was extremely difficult to cope with. All I wanted was to see my dear friend, Eileen, smile again. For the record, Leeny's Smile—she had a smile that could make you forget all the bad in the world. She had the most perfect, most radiant smile that literally displayed the core of her heart which was everything good.

One of the most challenging days of that year, actually, the hardest day of that year was the day of Nick's passing. November 17, 2009. I will never forget going to see Eileen after I got out of school; she had been at the hospital with him that day and was not at school. I remember being with her and the sound and vibrations coming from her phone, a blackberry. It was buzzing and ringing non-stop. People were sending condolences, apologies, and looking for confirmation that the news of Nick's passing was true. Could you imagine? Having to tell, explain and be the one to pass on the information or confirm that someone had just died, not just anyone, but Nick. Nick was not just anyone. This was Eileen's person. This was someone everyone in the school in town was rooting for.

As Eileen's friend at the time, I feel like I took on the sole responsibility of feeling like I had to make her happy again. I had to put the sparkle back in her eyes and that beautiful smile back on her face. The pressure I put on myself was something I soon realized was too much for someone my age to bear. I wanted to take away my friends' pain and suffering. I wanted to help make her whole again. We were only fifteen years old.

How could we be going through this? I know Eileen was the one who lost Nick, but I felt at the time I had lost Eileen. Again, I had never been through anything like this in my life, and I had never experienced such a monumental, life-changing loss. With that being said, I did not know how to process at the time, and I could not begin to understand or handle the way Eileen coped with losing Nick.

The days before Nick's passing and the days that followed, I very vividly remember Eileen being cold towards me, almost to the point of ignoring me or walking past me in the hallways in between classes. She would not say a word to me. I would go up to her to try and talk to her as we usually always connected during those passing periods, but I got nothing. How was this fair to me? What was going on with my friend? How could she treat me like this after all I had been good to her, supported her, and showed genuine care and concern for her well-being? I was a people pleaser. And the way Eileen was coping, the way she was making me feel without even being consciously aware, was something that broke me inside.

Being so young, I had no idea of the mental anguish Eileen was facing. How could I have known? How could I not have known? We were not educated in mental health, and it was not something that was talked about; there was no awareness in that regard at the time. So I was in the dark when it came down to what Eileen was really feeling emotional, what she was really battling. Eileen was never mean to me, never treated me poorly, but honestly, her absence and what felt like a rollercoaster of a friendship due to her emotions led me into something I now know as a slight depression. "Dark." That cloudy dark storm was still over us even after Nick passed and was free of any pain he was in and endured. I really struggled with understanding why Eileen was having to go through this terrible time in her life; why her? Why could it not have been me, instead? That is true friendship. Wishing you could take all the pain and sorrow out of someone else's life and go through it yourself just to save that other person.

So badly, I wanted nothing more than to see Eileen happy again. But, most importantly, I wanted to make her happy again. Hence, the pressure I put on myself to make that happen. But, as I said before, this pressure was something I soon couldn't bear. Eventually, it all caught up with me, and the toll it took on my mind, body, and soul were torturous. There were days I would lay in my room all day, all evening, and even on weekends when most were going out, I was left with bottomless emotions in my room. "Dark," I know I keep saying it, but that is how I felt inside.

All I could wonder and think about was why my friend hated me one day, I felt like she wanted nothing to do with me, but on other days she would just pretend like nothing ever happened like Nick never died, that our friendship was never strained. Then, finally, I remember conversing with my mom, and I explained how I was feeling and why. The toll the whole situation was taking on me, the dark feeling I was having. She comforted me and simply told me that I needed to take a break from Eileen; we probably needed space from one another for a little bit simply because of the depressive state I was in.

Again, looking back on it, it feels a little ridiculous that I felt so dark and depressed because of what I witnessed Eileen go through. What I was going through was and will never be compared to the proper caliber of what Eileen was dealing with. But I have to keep in mind, my feelings were real, true, and will always be validated. I could not possibly have known the ripple effect of Nick's passing because that is what it was, a ripple effect. Death hurts; losing people hurts. And at the time, the day Nick died, a massive part of the Eileen I knew died with him.

Eileen was trying to cope and handle her emotions and feelings on her own; it was evident. But, again, I wish so badly someone who professionally knew what was going on with Eileen could have educated me on mental illness, depression, and anxiety. I wish someone could have explained to me the way Eileen was acting towards me was simply her just trying to wrap her mind around what the hell was going on in her life; she was merely coping or trying to anyway. It had nothing to do with me. Yet, I put that pressure on myself still.

Looking back on that time in our lives, I now know how important mental health is and how much it really sucks to not feel in control of your mind and emotions. I wish I had seen the signs, and I wish I had known the signs and what to look for in others. The way you treat others can really reflect your genuine emotions, I know Eileen loved me, but the way she coped made me believe and think otherwise, which was again validated. If you were to ask Eileen today about any of this, I guarantee you she would probably tell you she has no recollection. Which is totally fair; she likely had blocked out every moment during that whole period and really was not even mentally present in those seriously dark times when I thought she may have been unhappy with me and our friendship.

When Eileen first reads this, it will probably make her sad, which is the last thing I want, but if I can share my view as an outsider watching what all she went through at that time in our lives and how she went through it, maybe it will help someone going through something similar. I hope people who are in my shoes will begin to understand what the other person is going through, read the signs, and offer support. We cannot blame ourselves for other people's happiness, and we cannot be the sole reason for someone's happiness no matter how much we want to help and be there.

From the moment I met Eileen, she was and will always be one of the most amazing friends I could have ever had. She is and will always be someone I genuinely care about. Yes, we have had to hurdle over some obstacles through our friendship, and at times we have lost touch over the years, but that's life. Somehow, we always manage to pick right back up where we last left off. That is friendship—no matter where we are in life, we have and will always remain friends.

To this day, Eileen continues to amaze me. She has an unending drive to keep pushing forward and always perseveres through everything that's been thrown at her in life. It is genuinely extraordinary where Eileen was and where Eileen is today, considering what all she has had to endure. I would have never been able to overcome the many challenges she has faced with the strength and grace she has displayed. I am and will always be unexplainably grateful to have Eileen in my life and to be able to call her one of my closest friends, and I love you, Leeny.

CHAPTER SEVEN

Hurricane Allison

A few months went by when I got a phone call from my friend from camp, Allison. Her diagnosis had made a turn for the worse. She was very sick. This is someone I had known for years, someone I adored. She had a smile that could light up a room and a personality to match. I told Allison I would come to visit her in the hospital at Texas Children's. I was at home, standing in my kitchen talking to my parents, when I got a call from Allison. I didn't answer and let it go to voicemail because I was a few minutes away from leaving and going to see her. Allison left me a voicemail, asking me to stop on the way to pick up a slushie and some sour candies. I smiled because that was so "Allison." I called her back and told her I would absolutely take care of that for her, and I would see her soon.

After grabbing the most enormous slushie size I could, I found numerous sour candies that I couldn't decide between getting—very indecisive—so I got them all. After parking, I lugged all of Allison's treats up to the ninth floor and slowly made my way to her room. At the time, I hadn't been back to the hospital since Nick's death, let alone on the cancer floor. I had a hard time reliving those steps, those emotions, and seeing his room number eleven. Finally, I found Allison's room; it was one of the big corner rooms. I walked in and found her lying in bed with who I remember was her father.

She looked like Nick did before he passed away. Unfortunately, the person I heard on the phone did not reflect who I was seeing. You see, there is this thing called "the honeymoon phase," where right before patients pass away, they are their usual selves for just a few minutes. I didn't think that phone call would be the last time I spoke to my dear friend.

Allison passed away on April 12, 2011. I attended her funeral, where I was given a journal entry Allison had written; it read, *"The labyrinth reminds me of the path kids with cancer have to take. There are so many unexpected twists and turns. It is easy to feel lost because you are always on the path alone. You want to get out, but you can't. All you can do is move forward and hope for an end. It's sad and lonely. You can try to take someone with you, but you can't. This labyrinth is your pathway and yours alone. Each kid with cancer sets out on this lonely journey by themselves. There are tears along the way and pain, but they keep moving forward to the circle in the center. The circle in the center seems to be different for different people. It's something you gain from the experience of wandering in a labyrinth. For me, the circle is confidence. At the end of my journey, I hope to reach confidence, confidence in myself, that I can beat whatever battle life throws at me, and confidence that I can find happiness even in a blanket of sadness. The labyrinth reminds me of a pathway, a pathway that kids just like me venture out onto every day."*

As the days and weeks passed following Allison's death, I relived losing Nick. I relived the grieving process that I was still going through. There wasn't in any way enough time to bounce back from three deaths in such a short period. I was slowly deteriorating. I continued obsessing over what I would eat if I ate at all. I started running with every chance I could get. I tried to control what I could in all the chaos life was throwing my way. I was trying to numb the endless pain.

I completely stopped communicating any sort of feelings or emotions to my family or friends. My mother would try to hug or comfort me, and I'd push her away every time, almost in fear I would break down and show weakness in how I felt. Whenever

Nick's name came up, I would completely shut down and go to my room to lie in bed and cry till I fell asleep. This was my life as a freshman in high school. When normal kids are thinking about parties, boyfriends, or high school functions, I was battling anxiety, depression, and suicidal thoughts. I carried these painful emotions with me every minute of every day and didn't get the help I needed because these were all feelings I kept all to myself, hidden from the world.

CHAPTER EIGHT

Hurricane Lilli

As a sophomore in high school, we had new next-door neighbors move in, the Curry's. A Mom, Dad, son, and daughter. Their daughter's name was Lili. When news that I was the "neighborhood babysitter" got out, I soon got asked to watch Lili and her brother when her parents would go on date nights or work functions. I loved watching kids. Kids are the best source of light in this world.

Soon after, Lili was diagnosed with Ewing's Sarcoma. She was just in elementary school. This type of cancer in the bones typically begins in your legs, pelvis, or arms. This was absolutely devastating news to hear. As with Nick, I talked to Lili about her fight. I encouraged her, and she began to look at me with hope knowing I was a cancer survivor. But, with that, for me came shame. How could anyone look up to me, not knowing the battles and struggles I was fighting mentally every second of every day?

Treatment started for Lili, and her mom was her biggest fan and advocate. One day Mrs. Curry invited me over for Lili's hair shaving party. Lili had the most beautiful silky blonde hair and the sweetest of smiles. The chemo was slowly making her hair fall out as it does to everyone. I walked over and sat in the kitchen while

Lili got her hair shaved off. Even when losing her beautiful blonde locks, that sweet girl had a smile on her face.

I will never forget participating in the "Relay for Life" that year, which is an event to raise awareness for cancer. The announcer asked all survivors to get on the track and take a lap together. I looked around and saw Lili standing on the outside of the track, and I walked over, reached my hand out to hers, and hand in hand took on that lap together. Another memory was during my senior year of high school. I was finally finished getting ready for my senior prom, and as I was walking out of the room, there was Lili, standing at the front door, waiting to see me all dolled up. It was such a treat, and I will never forget the shimmer in her eyes as she looked me up and down in my gown. Her eyes were so tired but still so incredibly full of life and fight. We snapped a picture together, and looking back at that picture now, being able to see her bright and beautiful smile is a picture I will carry with me forever. This picture is how I will never forget Lili.

As time went on and Lili's diagnosis became grimmer, I had to distance and detach myself. In hopes, when the time came for her to gain her angel wings, it would ease the pain in my heart and mind. I was wrong; whether I was as involved in her life or not, the pure and utter anguish I felt over any loss was unbearable. After a long lengthy battle with cancer, many rounds of treatments, and surgeries, Lili earned her angel wings and went to be with her Heavenly Father on August 4, 2016, at sixteen years of age. I cannot begin to explain the heartache and anguish I felt. The pain I felt for Lili, the pain I felt for her mother and family. And the pure disgust and shame I felt for being a survivor. I survived! I should be grateful for a second shot at life, for God picking me to live. But it was the complete opposite. I pleaded with God daily to take me instead of any child in this world. "Let me go to spare someone else" is what I pleaded with God daily.

"Lilli was an amazing person with a love for life. She also had an extraordinary gift to share her love for life in a way that brought out the best in others. She could relate to and connect with anyone from all

walks of life. She was fun and creative and compassionate, and a million other amazing qualities. She loved learning and doing everything… everything except fighting cancer. But she rarely complained about the fight in her five-year battle with Ewing's Sarcoma. And, goodness, was she a fighter. She battled through more chemo treatments, surgeries, radiation, and clinical trials in five years than anyone should have to in ten lifetimes, let alone a child. Even when she could barely breathe at the end, instead of settling for the good fight she had already given, she chose to push on toward more treatment. But when the end came, she peacefully settled into the loving arms of a host of angels who escorted her to Heaven. Her family, friends, and those who knew her were blessed by knowing her and miss her deeply. But we also know we will see her again. Knowing she will be there to welcome us gives us comfort."

Lili was an angel on earth—just like Allison, Tayler, and Nick. Just like every cancer patient I have ever known and had the pleasure of meeting. They were our angels here on earth, they are now our guardian angels watching over us, and they will continue to be our angels as we all pass on to Heaven. These children will all be at the gates of Heaven hand in hand, waiting for their loved one's arrivals, and they will be in perfect form, as we knew them before they were sick.

"Fear not, for I am with you; Be not dismayed, for I am your God. I will strengthen you, yes, I will help you, I will uphold you with my righteous right hand… For I, the Lord your God will hold your right hand, saying to you, 'Fear not, I will help you.'" Isaiah 41:10, 13.

CHAPTER NINE

Calmer Waters

In 2016, I was approached by Glenn Davis. He wanted me to participate in public speaking to youth soccer clubs known about my journey with cancer. These little soccer clinics were known as "Kick Cancer." Of course, I had known Glenn for years as he was near and dear to Nick. Now I was extremely hesitant at first, but I agreed to do it. I was then introduced to Freddy Reyes, a three-time cancer survivor, who would also speak about his battles with cancer. Little did I know we would become a trio to spend years together fundraising, raising awareness, and making a difference within the cancer community. I don't think I've ever told Glenn, but he changed my life by allowing and giving me a platform to share my story in a way that helped me cope with my losses and move forward with my life. And for that, Glenn, I will always be thankful you became a part of Nick's life and, in turn, my life.

When I would participate in these "Kick Cancer" camps, Glenn introduced me to a young man, Freddy. Freddy was also a cancer survivor. He not only beat cancer once, twice but THREE TIMES! Freddy was the definition of relentless. His fights against cancer were truly remarkable, a true testament to his strength and perseverance. Freddy was first diagnosed with Ewing Sarcoma on November 21, 2011. His tumor was located on his upper left tibia bone, right below his knee. In order to rid his body of cancer, they performed a procedure known as a Complete Knee Arthroplasty. Following the procedure, he endured chemo rounds from December of 2011 through July of 2012. Freddy then had his first relapse, meaning his cancer came out of remission in, summer of 2015. Doctors found a tumor behind Freddy's head after a week of excruciating headaches. In the process of scanning Freddy's body, the team of doctors discovered a small nodule in his lungs. This required four more months of chemotherapy.

I asked Freddy how being a cancer survivor had affected his day-to-day life. I wondered if it had impacted him as it had me. He went on to tell me, although he had survived the last couple rounds of chemotherapy and radiation blasts, he still has not passed his five-year mark, meaning his cancer has not been in remission for five years. The odds of his cancer coming back was a higher possibility because it had been less than five years. Something that had changed from treatment was his appetite. Chemotherapy affected his stomach, and he now had bad heartburn; his sleeping patterns varied, from being able to sleep like a baby to having nights where he would lie in bed and reminisce about having night shift nurses walk into his room every hour on the hour for vitals as he would try to get a good night's rest. Lastly, the knee surgery Freddy underwent had affected his walking. He was left with a slight limp in that leg that was barely noticeable, but those who saw him in his everyday life noticed it more than others. They had seen him as someone who was an athlete growing up who could run, jump and climb to someone who could no longer do those things.

Freddy and I often discussed how we felt about the public speaking Glenn always encouraged us to do. I always shared how I felt on the subject. Yes, it was hard to do, but I knew how helpful and impactful it was to the audiences we spoke with. Freddy shared those thoughts. He grew up not incredibly social, but this opportunity and platform we were given helped transform Freddy. It gave him and me both a voice, a voice to speak our cancer truth, and a voice to touch others going through the same things we had both been through. We also talked about the mental toll surviving cancer had on us. Being human, we are bound to deal with mental health struggles at different times in our lives for various reasons. Freddy had to deal with the anxiety and possibility of relapsing and has cancer returning. You see, the thing with cancer, it has no rules, no boundaries. Cancer can hide; cancer can sneak up on you when you least expect it. For someone with a higher chance of relapse, I cannot imagine having to live every day wondering if that cancer was somewhere hiding within my body. Freddy is newly married to the most beautiful person. She was made for Freddy. The pressure to provide for his wife and family weighs heavily on him, and when he most recently relapsed and was fighting cancer for the third time. That was when he mentally had the most challenging time.

Life after cancer for Freddy has been nothing less than a long road. To get where he is today and to have survived thus far has been more than a challenge. In the process of treatments and cancer in general, Freddy has reflected on all the good, including meeting countless numbers of patients in and out of the hospital. This life of his has taught him so many lessons, and it has led him to appreciate the little things in life and treasure all the big moments life has to offer. However, it has been a long road for Freddy and will continue to be because life is not over yet, and there will always be more challenges and hurdles to overcome. But there have been more victories than defeats. Freddy has found peace from cancer in knowing he is a fighter. He knows whatever he aspires for in life will not be handed to him but will be earned. Every day as a cancer survivor, Freddy encourages others to realize that to achieve and reach those unique parts of our lives, there will always be a chance of dying at some point; it is inevitable. Still, anything worth fighting for is dependent on our overall outlook on life. Our attitude is half the battle. So, choose always to fight and have that relentlessness.

Glenn, Freddy, and I would go to Texas Children's Hospital monthly to visit the cancer floor. We would deliver soccer balls and go room to room to visit with cancer patients and their families to share our stories as a symbol of hope. Without hope, what is there to fight for? I learned that my purpose here on earth was to symbolize hope and give faith to those fighting for their lives. The parents of patients would just stare at Freddy and me as we told them we were survivors. We were two individuals who probably had been treated in the same beds where these sons and daughters were lying. Some parents would cry, some would ask to hug us, some even asked to pray with them. At the end of our visit, parents, patients, and hospital staff always thanked us for doing there.

On one of our monthly visits, we walked the cancer floor, and when we rounded the corner, I saw the sweetest little boy riding in one of those push trucks; I will never forget it was fire truck red. As we approached this boy and his father, I got down on this sweet little boy's eye level, said hello, and asked if he wanted a soccer ball; he shook his head and said yes. His dad told Freddy, Glenn, and me his son's name was Sammy. Freddy, Glenn, and I introduced ourselves to Sammy's dad. Freddy and I spoke to him for a few minutes, and all I can remember is the utter exhaustion, sadness, and worry in that sweet man's eyes. We told him our stories, and he just looked at us with so much hope for his son. He asked us about our experiences with cancer, we swapped stories and went on our way to the next patient's room.

A few months later, I was updated that little Sammy had earned his angel wings on July 2, 2016. Hearing this news was all too familiar to me, and all I knew was that Freddy and I were going to that funeral and going to support Sammy's parents. The funeral was filled with family and friends. I will never forget sitting and looking at Sammy in his casket. Sammy rested in a red and blue superman casket. I thought to myself, Sammy was and will always be an actual superhero, and how fitting that casket was. When the service ended, I approached Sammy in his coffin and looked down, and I saw a sweet baby boy at peace. Now, why would God take a three-year-old from his family so abruptly? These are the questions I would ask myself. The only sense I can make of it? Sammy had a mission here on earth for those three years. He gave love, laughter and continued to spread hope. Maybe God needed a cute little three-year-old in Heaven with him.

* * * * *

"A limb has fallen from the family tree. I keep hearing a voice that says, Grieve, not for me. Remember the best times, the laughter, the song. The good life I lived while I was strong. Continue the heritage, and I am counting on you. Keep smiling, and surely the sun will shine through. My mind is at ease, and my soul is at rest. Remembering all how I truly was blessed. Continue traditions, no matter how small. Go on with your life, do not worry about falls. I miss you dearly, so keep up your chin. Until the day comes where we are together again."

Sammy's family was and will always be forever changed the day Sammy earned his angel wings. The pure devastation. The sadness and emptiness in their eyes as Freddy and I offered our condolences. Yet, despite all the pain and grief they must have felt, they made something good come out of their son's death. Sammy's parents founded a foundation in his honor in 2016. They made it their mission to help childhood cancer warriors fight the battle while raising cancer research funds. They created a foundation to honor their son's life. A tsunami turned their life upside down, yet they were able to turn darkness into light. That is something I will always find truly remarkable and an actual demonstration of strength.

For a few months, I had to take a break from our hospital visits. It seemed like the dark clouded storms were standing over me from time to time, and I learned I needed to take care of myself first before anyone else. You see, if you are not 100 percent mentally sound, how can you take care of others, let alone try to provide hope and comfort? Simply put, you cannot. And if you try to, you only end up hurting yourself in the process.

In the meantime, Glenn inspired me to start my own form of fundraising. Within my club soccer teams that I was coaching at the time, and the preschool I was teaching at, I started the "Kick Cancer Fundraiser." This fundraiser asked for donations of soccer balls that I would deliver to Texas Children's Hospital and monetary contributions to a local foundation to either "The Curing Children's Cancer Fund" or the "Snowdrop Foundation." These were both foundations that benefited families and children affected by cancer and Texas Children's Hospital. Although Glenn had introduced me to these organizations, he was my biggest supporter of the work I was doing. Glenn even hosted me on his radio show, "Soccer Matters," and this gave me a bigger platform to talk about the fundraiser and its mission. The outpour of love and support was terrific. All I wanted to do was touch as many people as I could and make a difference in the world, while also hoping to inspire others to get involved and bring awareness to childhood cancer.

Chapter Ten

Colorful Waters

Growing up in the Mormon faith, "gay" or "lesbian" was not a part of my vocabulary. It was not something common or talked about. But, as I got older, I realized I had a gay uncle, and my oldest brother, Anthony, was also a part of the LGBTQ+ community.

It wasn't until middle school when I realized Anthony was gay. He was eight years older than I was and in high school at the time when a boy approached me in the hallway during school hours and said to me, "Is your brother Anthony gay"? I was so shocked and taken back it took me a few seconds to gather my thoughts. Finally, I replied with, "Why? Do you want me to give him your number?" Although this boy was more taken back by my response than I was with his question, I turned and walked to my next class with a smile on my face.

Anthony and I were always close growing up; he would play Barbies with me in the hospital—he was always better at dressing them, and I found it funny my Barbie heads never matched their bodies because he would switch them around. But I'll tell you what—when Anthony worked on those dolls, and they were by far the best-dressed Barbies I had ever seen. Anthony was the most creative, sweetest, and caring big brother I could have ever asked for. Almost weekly, I remember Anthony creating a "stage" with blankets and tables in our upstairs game room and sometimes our bedrooms, where he would transform the space and turn it into a fashion show. And these were not just any fashion shows. These were productions! And Anthony was the mastermind behind it all.

Of course, me being me, I hated these days. Anthony would use me as his "model," and I know he probably wished at the time he had a more girly sister. I hated hair and make-up, changing clothes, and especially disliked walking the runway, even if just in front of my parents, who would almost always be filming. Yes, these are on film. I bet you wish this book could feature video footage; luckily, for me, that is impossible.

My point in talking about my dear brother Anthony—yes, he is gay. I am proud to have a strong brother who endured more teasing and taunting by humans than anyone I know for simply just being himself. Unfortunately, people that are within the LGBTQ+ community are doing just that, being themselves. But I have learned you cannot change anyone, but you can educate them. And if they are open to hearing, you can make a difference in the mindset they may have or had towards that specific community and come out with a better understanding of the fact those people are just humans themselves. Love is love. Knowledge is power. Accepting someone who differs from you is like a miracle in itself.

In high school, after Nick's passing, I did date a few boys. But I never did anything past kissing them. Why? I just had no interest. There was not anyone who identified as a part of the LGBTQ+ community that I was aware of, so it just went right over my head. I feel like I was more preoccupied with my mental battles, friends being sick, school, and soccer than dating. The thing with losing Nick, he was the best young man I knew and would ever know. Anyone I dated, I always compared them to him. Was that fair of me? No, absolutely not. But I loved Nick with everything in me, and that is something challenging to let go of or begin to move on from, no matter what amount of time passes by.

In my freshman year of college, I met someone I really began to have feelings for. The only thing was that it was a woman. This was an uncharted territory that was scary, exciting, and nerve-wracking all at the same time. I kept this to myself and a secret for a good time before feeling like I should tell my mom. See, mom was my best friend, and I told her everything. So, one day I was walking to a class, and I gave her a call. We had our everyday small talk, and I told her I had to tell her something, and I know that caused anxiety for her in itself. "I think I am like Anthony," and this was received with silence and confusion.

My mama's vision for me was to always be with a man like my father. A provider, someone with strong morals and values who would always take care of me. She had a vision for her princess. I will never fault her for that. So, her hearing I was in a transitional period in my sexuality took her back. She also feared I would come home for the holidays with a buzz cut and wearing cargo pants. You might be thinking, "What irrational thoughts," but I found it quite hilarious.

The difference between Anthony and me, Anthony came dancing out of the womb. He loved fashion, he was creative in all things, and it was more apparent for those around him to understand him being gay. I am not saying everyone who identifies with being a gay male is into fashion by any means. Now with me, I was not highly girly. But I was girly enough. I was more of a sporty girl who would rather be in sports clothes than dresses, hated wearing heals and all that comes with being a girl. For example, when I had high school dances, Anthony picked out my dresses. Anthony picked my shoes. Anthony decided what my hair and makeup would look like. Anthony even brought in people to do my hair and make-up or sometimes even did it himself—he was damn good at it too. I definitely did not appreciate the work he and my mom put into my appearances for those events at the time, especially when Anthony would make me go to tanning beds or get spray tans since I always had terrible soccer clothes and shin guard tan lines. But they are memories I will never forget and cherish.

I will also never forget walking in one of Anthony's charity fashion shows benefiting cancer research. I was so anxious to participate and was heavily dealing with the guilt of being a survivor and even being given the opportunity to walk in this show. I am sure I appeared to be a brat in Anthony's eyes, which I would prefer over him knowing how I was feeling. In the end, I bared through the hair, the makeup, and the multiple outfit changes and walked in this fashion show. I actually enjoyed myself and cherished the memories of Anthony and me backstage laughing and joking as we prepped for the following walks. I guess my point is, being gay does not define you; loving whoever you choose to love does not define you. Your profession does not define you. Anthony is talented in what he does, he loves who he loves, and he overcame any obstacle or adversity that came with it; that is what defines a person.

Being a part of the LGBTQ+ community has been something for a long time, I would not claim. See, in my mind, I am who I am. I would not define myself by who I love. It just did not make sense to me. I am proud to love my partner. I am proud to be a strong lesbian woman. I am proud to stand strong for those who are in the same stage of life in their sexuality and for those still navigating their way through the process. Because at the end, who are we if we are not proud of who we really are? That acceptance, that self-love is more important than anything.

This year I decided to share with my eleven-year-old soccer team that I was in a relationship with a woman. This was my first. I never shared my private life with my professional life. But these girls were so adamant about talking and asking about my "boyfriends" that I never confirmed or denied I had. So again, I called them in at the beginning of practice; furthermore, they asked me if I got married that weekend as I had to miss a game for a wedding. I smiled and told them, "Well girls, I have bad news for you," now, looking back, I should not have said "bad news" because it was not bad news. I then stuttered and fumbled over my words, trying to find the proper, age-appropriate wording. "You know how some people like girls? And some people like boys?" they responded with "Yes." "Well, I like girls, and I have a partner." Again, I heard some "I knew it" and some gasps. Then one of my sweet players slapped her cheeks with her hands, looked at me with her sweet, innocent green eyes, and said, "Wait, you, you are a lesbian?!" I could not help but burst out in laughter. That is the thing about working with children, and they are so full of love, innocence, and acceptance in all aspects of life. They represent something I hope most grown adults can learn from.

Adversity. The difficulties of one's life. I preach to every player I have ever encountered always to show resilience in the face of adversity. Whether it be in a game, practice, or especially in life. My life has been an uphill battle in which I have displayed an incredible amount of resilience in every face of adversity. The waves of my struggles with cancer led me to all other streams of my life. I had to overcome the hardships of life. I had to overcome cancer, but I wouldn't have learned these vital lessons and shared these experiences with others without that fight. I hope these challenges I have overcome can help someone facing similar circumstances and, ultimately, make a difference.

Chapter Eleven

Wavelength

I played soccer growing up, never really thinking about my lifelong career in the sport. It was fun playing with friends in the recreational leagues. My older brother Josh played soccer as well. As he got older and his talents stood out on the field, he progressed into the Club Soccer world. I soon followed. This is where my skills developed, and I grew into a dependable player on the field to my teammates and coaches.

The summer going into my freshman year of high school, I was invited to play on another club team and go on a summer "soccer tour" across Germany, France, and Austria. This was a trip of a lifetime, and my parents were more than encouraging about going on this two-week-long excursion. This is where my true love and passion for soccer developed. This is where I learned how much I truly loved the game of soccer, not just because Nick loved it, but because I loved it. Every day we ventured into cities of Germany, France, and Austria. We hiked, explored, and visited historical sites, and the best part was our nightly exhibition matches against local soccer teams. The skill, the style of play, the competitiveness was something that changed my outlook on soccer. I have carried this into the way I coach and the style of play I implement into my teams. You see, this coach I played for on this team believed in me; he believed in my abilities to perform as a player and a leader on the field. He is ultimately the reason why I picked up coaching years later.

After every game, the opposing team we played would host our team for dinner. Most dinners consisted of a form of Schnitzel; I would say it is an acquired taste. Nonetheless, it was intriguing to learn about the different cultures, languages, and meeting new people. The hospitality was terrific. I will never forget after matches when we would head to the locker room, which always had a group head of showerheads; we American girls would wear our swimsuits under our uniforms, so when it was time to shower, we would just take our uniforms off and shower in our swimsuits. Well, after one of our last games, we all did the usual, grabbed our shower stuff, and started to shower in our swimsuits. To our surprise, a door opened, and the opposing team walked in; it was a communal locker room shower. They did not walk in swimsuits, and they walked in naked. Oh my gosh, my teammates and I did not know what to do. Still to this day, those memories make me laugh.

Now going into my freshman year in high school, I tried out for the soccer team; for whatever reason, the varsity team coach did not see me as a fit for the team, and I was placed on the JV-A soccer team. I was highly discouraged by this but kept my head up and accepted my spot on the JV team. This was a team I became a leader on, nominated as a Captain. This is also where I was fortunate enough to have a coach who truly loved and believed in me with all his being—Coach Filson. Lucky for me, he also was my history teacher. This man was one of a kind. The way he believed in me was the same way he believed in every single one of his players and students. He encouraged us to be the best version of ourselves, be leaders in society, and always do our best to make a difference in the world.

Sophomore year came, I made the varsity team. My coach was nowhere near the kind of coach I had in Coach Filson. I kept my head down and did the best I could, but my work primarily went unnoticed. By the end of my year, I tore my lateral and medial meniscus in my right leg, which was my dominant leg. At our end-of-season evaluation, I was told by this grown man that I likely wouldn't come back from this injury, that I wasn't big enough or fast enough for this varsity team. I left his office in disbelief. How could I be so successful on my club team but not be good enough for a high school team? That goes to show you the impact a coach can have on the mental aspect that comes with playing sports. I kept my head up. I didn't return to play high school soccer and decided to focus on my club team in hopes of playing collegiate soccer.

By my junior year, I was contacted by multiple colleges in and out of the state. I participated in college showcase tournaments with my club team. I made a verbal commitment to play soccer on scholarship at Queens University of Charlotte in North Carolina, the same school my older brother Josh was attending and also playing soccer at. I was the only one in my high school class to go on to play collegiate soccer. That was the most effective form of validation I could have ever had regarding my high school varsity coach. I was always a talented enough player to reach a higher stage.

In August of 2012, I was off to Charlotte, NC. I had a rigorous soccer practice and game schedule while trying to maintain a healthy educational balance. My parents had just dropped me off at the fields while they headed out to explore my new city. This was my first day of soccer practice at the collegiate level. My new coach split the team in two towards the end of the training, and we began a scrimmage. I was playing a forward position, and the ball was passed back to the opposing team's defender, so I chased after it. I was about six feet from the defender when she went to clear the ball, and it knocked me on the side of my head. I stumbled while trying to walk the hit-off before being escorted off the field and taken to the athletic trainers on staff at the school. About fifteen minutes later, my parents picked me up to head to the doctor, and I was later diagnosed with a concussion. I was out of training for the next month or two. Being out of training at the beginning of the season was tough. You lose any chance at a starting position, and you lose your stamina; you lose confidence. When I finally came back to the field, not a few months later, I tore the lateral and medial meniscus on my left leg. I was devastated. This is where I was left with the decision of medically retiring from collegiate soccer.

Soccer meant more to me after Nick's passing. Soccer was something we both loved and shared a passion for. But Nick's love for the sport was something out of this world, which made me love it that much more. After Nick passed away, I promised myself I would always stick with soccer for him, whether that meant playing or coaching. During the first year after Nick died- with almost every soccer game I played- at some point during the warmup or game, I would look up at the sky, and I would see a white bird. I always thought it might have been a dove, but I am no bird expert. Regardless, every time I saw this "dove," I felt my Nick with me on that soccer field, and it pushed me that much harder. Seeing that bird gave me hope that one day I would be reunited with my dear friend.

Chapter Twelve

Sinking Ship

In 2013, my mental struggles began to overtake me. I wasn't functioning at all. On my first day of community college, I stayed in bed. No one was home that day. I just simply did not have the will to get up. I cried and cried as I thought of ending my life and thinking of being reunited with all my lost friends. I prayed and prayed and saw no other options.

I found a bottle of pills, and slowly I used water to swallow them—one after another. As the bottle came to become empty, I went back to bed and just hoped all the pain I was feeling would be gone and that I could be free. I soon after fell into a deep sleep only to wake up that evening. That night I woke up throwing up and feeling awful. I texted one of my close friends and asked him if he would come over. I cried and confided in him about what I had done, and he told me I had to tell my parents and get to the hospital to make sure everything was alright. Reluctantly, I opened my bedroom door, walked down the stairs, and approached my parents. I told my parents what I had done, and they furiously took me to the Emergency room.

Luckily, I hadn't taken enough medicine to need my stomach pumped. But because of what I did, I had to be sent to a state psychiatric hospital for forty-eight hours. I'll never forget what my father said to me that night, as it was my mother's birthday at midnight. "A little girl is fighting for her life right next door to our house, and you're at home doing this!" All I could do was cry—his comment pierced my heart, but I will never hold that against my father. I hadn't communicated my feelings for years. I kept everything locked away in a vault.

How would he have known how those words would affect me? How could he have possibly known? The simple answer, he could have never known what demons I had been fighting; no one could have known.

This hospital I was sent to was like how I remembered Texas Children's Hospital when I was little, dark and grey. It was lonely. It was scary. See, I knew I did not belong with those people in that hospital. People with schizophrenia, Bipolar patients, people who would rock back and forth talking to themselves. It was traumatic. Yes, I was suffering from mental health issues, but it was not the same way those people were suffering. I might be wrong, but that's how I felt. When my parents would come to visit me, I would be so relieved to see them, but all I could do was cry. I was in a mental jail for my safety.

When I returned from the psychiatric hospital, my parents, who I can only imagine how helpless and confused they must have felt, signed me up for intense Dialectical Behavior Therapy (DBT). The main goals for anyone receiving this form of treatment are to learn basic skills to focus on living in the moment, coping with stress in healthy ways, learning to regulate emotions, and improving interpersonal relationships. This was a life-changing treatment. This is where I met Becks. This woman was patient, kind, and compassionate beyond belief. She helped me try to overcome the past traumas of my life. She laughed with me, and sometimes she even cried with me even when I wouldn't cry myself. The trauma and memories I shared with Becks would sometimes bring her to tears as I spoke; I think she just could not wrap her mind around someone my age enduring so much, or maybe she could empathize and obviously knew how to feel her emotions when she was feeling them. I was the opposite; no matter how badly my body wanted to push those tears out, I would not allow it. I did not want to show a sign of weakness or instability. When in all actuality, that might have been a bit insane in itself. But Becks soon helped me understand and see that crying was a good thing; crying was a healthy way to cope with my emotions and a way to move on and heal from my past. You see, bottling in our feelings is what will ultimately hurt us in the long term.

Becks taught me how important being mindful was, living in the present moment. *"The practice of mindfulness is the practice of love itself."*[2] She always told me and encouraged me to "Live a Life Worth Living ". Anyone who loved me could see I was stuck in the past. I was taught skills to stay in the moment and understand where I was at that exact moment in time. Next was the power of validation; knowing my feelings regarding my past was more than valid and was certainly something I didn't know I needed. But I did. I needed to know why I felt the way I felt and reassure myself that those feelings were real and the backup of "Yes, that did happen to me, and that is why I feel the way I do." It was one thing to be taught these life skills and to practice them daily; this was something I struggled with.

---

2   Thich Nhất Hạnh and Mayumi Oda, *Touching Peace: Practicing the Art of Mindful Living* (Parallax Press: 2009), 47.

Chapter Thirteen

Drowning

Two years after my first attempt at ending my life, I continued struggling with survivor's guilt. After being with that person for over a year and living together, I had just gotten broken up with. My attempt was not due to this person leaving me. See, I had experienced so much loss that even a breakup that was so incredibly overdue, to me, was another loss that felt like a death.

"Many of us, although alive, are not really alive because we are not able to touch lives in the present moment."[3] I was alive. But I was not living in the present moment; I was forever stuck in my past of pain and loss with no chance of moving on and forward with my life without peace. You see, when you are able to live in the present moment, you are then able to find your life.

It's not that I didn't want to live; I very much did. But the truth is, I wasn't functioning anymore. My therapist Becks tried to get me to come in and talk with her, and I am sure she sensed something more was going on with me. She made me promise I would not hurt myself; she told me to give it a week and assured me I would feel better; I did just that. I kept my promise and waited a week. And

---

3   Hạnh, *Touching Peace*, 3.

on the eighth day, I realized the pain and feelings I was feeling were not ever going to go away. My mind would never feel the peace of all the survivors' guilt I was enduring.

The pain, the loss, the grief I felt were too much for me to understand and cope with. In the summer of 2014, I lived alone, and I was on medication for anxiety and depression. I had a three-month supply of both. And one night, I decided I had endured enough. My family was on vacation, and I knew they'd be gone. I took all the pills, gagging, my body fighting me every time I swallowed. I took a shower, I put on a t-shirt my dad had gotten me from Florida, and my pajamas which were a matching set I shared with my mom. I kissed my dogs. I got in bed and took a video telling my family individually how much I loved them and how sorry I was.

You see, this was not anyone's fault. I was coaching youth soccer just the day before, and no one could have seen this coming—the night before, I played in an adult soccer league. In my mind, I was at peace with my decision. For me, this couldn't have been prevented. My life up to that point was a series of traumatic events I just could not cope with. As a matter of fact, I quite plainly didn't have time to cope with these events that came one after another, like ocean waves crashing over me. I wasn't living. I was stuck in a world of pain, anguish, and pure devastation. My heart was shattered into a million tiny pieces that I was not strong enough to put back together. Something no one but I would understand.

My boss at the time called my emergency contact, which was my mom, and let her know I didn't show up for work that morning and that they couldn't get a hold of me. My mom, dad, and little brother were in New Jersey at the time visiting family, so my mom contacted my brother, Josh, who was in town. My brother drove out to my apartment to find the door locked, called the property manager to open the door, who then realized I had locked the bolt as well. Eventually, someone was able to open the door, and a team of paramedics found me unconscious in my apartment. I had cuts, bruises, and broken toes due to seizing for hours before anyone found me.

I woke up in a hospital bed with tubes in my mouth and my family surrounding me, from what I remember. All I could do was cry. I don't know if I cried out of relief at being able to see my family again or sadness that I was unsuccessful once again. I couldn't talk but instead reached out for each family member, one after another, to hold their hands almost as if I were trying to say, "I love you, and I'm sorry."

I spent a little over a week in Ben Taub Hospital, located in the Houston Medical Center downtown, where I slowly recovered mentally and physically. One visit I had during my stay that I remember particularly well was when my therapist came to see me over the past few years. This was someone who I adored and genuinely loved—Becks. She sat by my bedside and talked with me. We both cried. She was there as a source of comfort and let me know I could and would come back from this point in life. She reminded me to focus on being mindful, present in the current moment, that my feelings were validated. She had taught me skills to help my quality of life that I just couldn't implement on my own at the time.

This second attempt affected everyone involved in my life because I was one step away from being out of this world. My parents sent me to a facility in Houston with daily therapy, coping, and group works with other adults battling similar issues. As much as I hated being "locked up," I think it gave my family peace of mind that I was getting the help I so desperately needed. In addition, my sweet dad came to visit me every single day during visiting hours. He would offer me words of encouragement, hold me while I fought back the tears, and just let me know how much he loved and supported me.

That treatment facility is where I was able to get regulated with medication to help balance my mood. I can honestly say that the team of counselors and doctors sent me back into the world better than I was when I arrived. However, my family was hesitant and concerned when I was released after a week, and it wasn't until I came home that I realized the toll of my actions, specifically on my parents. My father began running obsessively every day. My mother left, unannounced, for days. My actions affected her most severely.

CHAPTER FOURTEEN

Lifeguard

In my family, I have a mom, a dad, and three brothers. My oldest brother is Anthony, he is six years older than me, then comes Joshua, who is three years older than me, and last there is Jake, who is four years younger than me. Of any of my brothers, Jake probably had to see me struggle more than Anthony and Josh since we were under the same roof. Each of them has their own recollection of my life and struggles and their effects on them as individuals. Jake was brave enough to share his version of my second suicide attempt and his overall outlook with me. Jake is a protector; he is intuitive to others' feelings. At times my little brother was my lifeguard. On my bad days, he was there to talk to me, and he was a shoulder to lean on and always provided me with words of encouragement that ultimately gave me hope.

* * * * *

At sixteen years of age, I remember Eileen had just got back from queen's university of charlotte after a year of attending and playing soccer for the college. She was enrolled at the local community college to take courses to stay on track with her classes to stay. I remember I was sitting in the movie room one evening, and her friend Alan came over. He went into Eileen's room, and not long after, he went into the room with me and simply said, "you guys really need to be there for Eileen". I had no idea what the hell he was talking about. I was sixteen, you know? At that age, relationships with your siblings are kind of just touch and go, and it's hit or miss if you are friends with your siblings; we have good and bad days. Again, I had no idea what he was talking about. Then Alan went on to tell me that Eileen had taken pills; this left me feeling so confused. I walked out of the movie room, stepped into the hallway that led to Eileen's room, and could see her propped up under the covers and just the look on her face; she looked messed up. The next thing I knew, my parents were taking her to the ER, where she was examined and later taken to a psychiatric facility run by the state.

After that first attempt to end her life, I will never forget the constant feeling of being on high alert and always being so scared and worried that Eileen would try to end her life again. Whenever she and my mom would bicker or argue, Eileen would often leave the house, and I remember constantly feeling that scared and worriedness in the pit of my stomach. I always felt like we needed to follow her and make sure she would not repeat herself. Like I said, high alert.

But you know, things eventually got better for Eileen; she began doing things she loved, like coaching soccer. That was when she just started out coaching. She was also nannying at the time; anything to do with kids was right up Eileen's alley. So then summer going into my senior year rolled around. I was eighteen years old. Eileen was doing great, so everyone, including myself, thought. Eileen had her own place, and she seemed happy; she had come out as a lesbian; she was just living her life.

That summer, my mom, dad, my best friend, and myself went on a vacation together to visit our extended family in New Jersey. I wanted to be a navy seal at the time, so I was in tip-top shape; I am talking, swimming, and running every morning, just in a great place mentally and physically. It was a great time in my life. Where we were visiting in New Jersey, it was super hilly with open fields, so every day we were there, I could just go on great runs surrounded by nature, the pure feeling of just freedom and enjoying life. A few days later, we packed up and drove down to the shore to stay in a beach house with all of our extended family on my dad's side. These were cousins, aunts, and uncles I had not seen in years; it was really special to be able to spend time with everyone again

Then one day, my family and I all went out by the water to go "crabbing." We were having such a great time with one another. Out of nowhere, my mom started to freak out. She was hysterical. We could not make out what she was trying to say. "Eileen is in the ICU." That is when I learned my sister tried to kill herself once again. This was when I discovered my sister might not make it this time. It was dire. I remember walking back into the beach house; happiness and laughter turned into sadness, worry, and disarray. I remember going into the room I had been staying in and just praying. I prayed so hard. I begged and pleaded with God to let Eileen live.

Not one person slept that night. My dad booked us on the next flight back to Houston, Texas. As soon as we got back to Houston, we drove to the Ben Taub Hospital. to the hospital, where we saw Eileen for the first time. Doctors told us she had stabilized. I remember she smelt like blood, and she was not making a lot of sense; she was hysterical in a way. She looked broken, and she just looked so broken inside. I remember talking to her and just promising her the world and saying anything I could to make her want to stay, and it was so tough. Finally, I remember one of the doctors coming in to realign her dislocated toes and hearing her cry out in pain. It was not a good time.

Next, my parents, brothers, and I drove over to Eileen's apartment. As I walked in for the first time ever, all I could think was how proud I was of her; her home was so lovely and well put together, how far she had come. Then reality would hit, and the feeling of utter sadness after remembering and realizing all that had transpired in the last forty-eight hours. How did we not see this coming? How did we not know?

My dad and I were left to pack up all of Eileen's belongings and move them out of the apartment as my parents were moving her home to help in her recovery. I walked into her bedroom for the first time and saw from the walls how much she struggled, how much her body fought back from what she had put into it. There was blood all over the walls. Blood from seizing and her feet banging her toes into the walls, that's how she ended up with two broken toes, and the rest were dislocated. It just looked like a crime scene, honestly. I remember it being such a typical hot summer day for Houston. I remember going up and down flights of stairs box after box loading up the moving truck with my dad. Finally, I walked back into the apartment with only one box left to take down, where I saw my dad through the doorway in Eileen's bedroom. He was standing with his hands upon the wall, head on his forearm next to the spot on the wall that showed most of Eileen's blood and struggle. His eyes were closed. It was the first time in my life, in eighteen years, that I had ever seen my father emotional. This was the first time I had ever seen my father break. This was the person I always knew as upbeat, someone who demonstrated nothing but strength, and such a positive person with the best outlook on any given situation. Seeing my father break is something that will be embedded in my mind forever.

A week later, Eileen was out of the hospital and taken to a private psych hospital my parents had checked her into. We went as a family to see Eileen. I remember all the people there, people going through their issues, and I just remember thinking my sister did not belong here. Eileen seemed like she was getting better and back to her usual self. Naturally, she was even making recommendations on how to make the facility run better; Eileen had always had a natural ability to lead. It was refreshing to hear.

When we got back to the house from visiting Eileen, my mom went into her room and packed a suitcase. She came out with her bag and let us know she was leaving. Although, at the time, I remember being so angry with her, now I know and understand that was so much for her to deal with, it was tough for everyone, and we all had to find our own way of processing and to find our own peace. She just needed that week away to cope with what was going on in our lives at the time.

From then on, things got better for Eileen. She began doing the things she loved. She continued coaching soccer and started teaching; she was just doing all the things that made her happy. Not long after, it was time for me to leave for college at Texas State. I decided I no longer wanted to be a Navy Seal. I realized that when you go off to college, you really start to see things differently; you see the world differently. I *began to question everything I had seen and learned. I went through ups and downs. During those times, I would be down and wondering if there was still good in the world; I would see all the good things my sister was doing on social media. I saw her giving back to hospitals where she frequently volunteered her time. I was seeing Eileen doing public speaking in front of kids who were going through cancer treatments and just being that light for them, showing them they could get through it.*

Those are the things that always brought a huge smile to my face and always made me so incredibly proud of her. Eileen had just come so far along, and she was doing so incredibly well. I am so pleased to say, Eileen has been doing phenomenal ever since. I do not doubt in my mind she has an everyday mental battle. I know she battles hard. But the difference from then to now is that Eileen had learned to cope with daily life and struggles. I am very grateful that she has found that peace within herself.

For those going through similar struggles as my sister, you can get through this for anyone in the world. This is a story of hope; take every day one day at a time, and always remember better days are ahead.

Chapter Fifteen

Ripple Effect

When I was sick with cancer, my mom and dad were by my side every step of the way, my biggest cheerleaders, my best friends. My parents fought just as much for my life as I did. The strength they demonstrated and showed me gave me power. I think that's why as I got older, I never wanted to show a sign of weakness in fear my mom and dad would notice. I saw them struggle when I was sick, and I'd hear them sniffle and cry as I was going to sleep. And the worry and heartache they felt when doctors would come into my room. I remember the sadness in their eyes as I would have to go into procedures and hear me scream and cry out for either one of them, if not both. How helpless they must have felt. My mother and father were just as much a fighter in my diagnosis as I was.

Now my parents have to see me in the mental state, the desperate and dark feelings I was having. Realizing their daughter, a cancer survivor, continued to fight for her life day in and day out from mental health, and it must have been just as hard. My dad was stressed; I think I aged him a few years due to my state and actions. He was scared and worried he would lose his little girl; he and my mother both were. My dad began excessively running. I think that was his way of coping with what was going on. My mom was angry, and she did not understand. She left soon after I returned from the treatment center. I think it was easier for her to go and cope on her own time and with space. They could not fathom the thought of me being out of their lives, especially at my hand after all we had been through. And for that, I will always be remorseful and sorry. After all, we had endured together, and I did not intend to hurt my family, especially my parents.

My relationships with my brothers all seemed to shift as well. My oldest brother Anthony was someone I regularly would see, have dinners, sleepovers with—I loved spending time with him and his husband, Richard. However, after my second suicide attempt, Anthony stopped talking to me. He never reached out to check in; we stopped spending time together. This bothered me deeply. About a year later, Anthony and I had a conversation where he explained to me that the situation I created was just too much for him to handle. He did not recognize the person I had become at that time. That he couldn't get close to me, knowing I could try to end my life again at any time. I put that fear in my brother without even realizing it.

Next was Joshua, my second oldest brother. Josh and I never really seemed to be on the same page growing up. Looking back on it, we had so much in common and were more similar than I realized. We both loved soccer, and he was a phenomenal player, which I always admired about him. Regardless of our differences, I loved my brother, and I wish I would have told him that more. Thinking about the mental toll my accident must have had on him and his life as he was the one who found me and might be the reason why I am alive today is something that haunts me to this day—having to walk into my bedroom and find his little sister covered in blood from seizing into the walls and furniture, seeing my toes all broken and mangled looking. Having to call my parents, who were out of state, to tell them they needed to be on the first flight back to Texas. I can only imagine the burden and heartache I have embedded in his mental state.

Lastly, my little brother Jacob. Jake is four years younger than me. I'm his big sister. I'm supposed to be someone he looks up to and can learn from. While I hope now, I am that person, I know back then I simply could not be. And I hope with that, he understands. Jake was just a baby when I got sick with cancer, and he was just a teenager trying to navigate through high school when I began having much heavier issues in life. Jake always offered words of encouragement when he could. He always told me I could bounce back from anything. I should have been the one supporting him, not the other way around. Jake has always been good to me, and for that, I will always be thankful. I only wish one day I could provide him with as much love and support he showed me in my most dire time in life.

You see, every decision you make in life has consequences, both good and bad. Your actions will always have a ripple effect on those around you and those involved in your life. When making my final decision to end my life, I cried, knowing I would hurt my family by dying. But in those last days and moments leading up to it, I was in so much pain and misery that I felt I had no other option. I knew this would hurt my family and loved ones, but I wanted peace and solace so severely. I wanted to be in Heaven, utterly free from all mental anguish. I wanted to be reunited with all my angels. Fortunately for me, I was given another shot at life.

In the months following my incident, my parents began going to NAMI classes. This was a course that better-equipped family members of loved ones suffering from mental health issues and disorders. My parents worked so hard, they never missed a class, and they did all of this to learn how to best assist in my recovery. They did this together because they wanted to support me in the best and most helpful way possible. Because of the completion of this course, we were able to communicate better, and they were able to understand me, my emotions, and the way my brain was working at the time. This was a beautiful expression of their love for me.

Chapter Sixteen

Life Raft

Months later, I immersed myself in coaching soccer. I coached for the Houston Dynamo Youth programs, which introduced me to a local private school, St. Thomas Episcopal. After seeing me coach, I was soon offered a position as a soccer coach on campus for the youth programs. Not long after I started, I was approached by the preschool director and offered a position as an assistant preschool teacher. Life was slowly coming together for me, and I couldn't have been more excited and blessed for the opportunity.

What I've learned from coaching and teaching preschool is that children are resilient. Children are the light in a world full of darkness. They offer so much love, purity, and innocence to life's imperfections. Coaching and teaching children have been and will always be the biggest blessings of my life. Surrounding myself with so much love was the best therapy or medication I had ever or will ever have.

Next came coaching club soccer. I never knew I could love thirteen wild little kiddos as much as I loved that first team I coached. The spunk, the sass, the skill, and devotion to making me proud is something I will forever be grateful for. We went on to win the state tournament our first year. That group of girls and parents stuck with me for three years. The support and love I felt were something I will never forget. You see, I firmly believe certain people are placed in your life for a reason. This group of girls put a smile on my face, made me laugh, and made me feel loved even on the hardest of days.

The relationships formed between the players and the parents and families on that specific team are relationships I will be forever grateful for—one in particular—the "L" Family. I still keep in touch with this family to this day.

Toni and Joe are two remarkable, giving, and the most supportive parents I know. Toni was someone I could lean on, go to for advice, and she was just a good human to have in my life. This was someone who supported me 110 percent in every decision I made through the years, and she offered her motherly wisdom when it came to my personal life and always praised me for the hard work I put into my coaching career. Toni once told me, "You belong in the college coaching world." She praised me for my efforts as a coach, and she encouraged me; she most importantly believed in me. Joe, what I loved about Joe was his utter bluntness in telling it how it is. Like Toni, he always offered advice when needed, supported me when I needed it most, and always hooked me up with the best Houston Rodeo concert tickets. This was a family I spent a lot of time with off the soccer field—dinners, sporting events, and at-home hangouts. They have three beautiful daughters: Riley, Ellie, and Reese. Luckily, at some point over the years, I had the pleasure of coaching all three of them. But first, I started coaching Ellie, and she was on my team that won state in our first year. Ellie was a remarkable player; I knew that she was naturally gifted within the first session of coaching her. She saw the field; she knew when to release the ball and when to take players on one-on-one to the goal. The skill, the consistency, and the pure love for the game of soccer is something so rare to come by in players, especially at such a young age. Yet, these qualities Ellie possessed never let up, and she continues to thrive on the field. To this day, I stand by saying she has a very bright soccer career ahead of her.

Now a few years later, I find myself living in Northern Kentucky. I approached Russel, the Director of Coaching for a successful "boutique" soccer club in Cincinnati, Ohio. Russel is British and has a very thick accent, a very tall man, and a redhead. You cannot miss him. He is the coolest. In our first phone interview, I could barely make out what he was saying but got the gist: to come out to the facility and run a session like an interview. So I went out to what we know as the "Futsal Factory" where my interviewer met me. I ran a successful session with a group of girls I had never met and, not long after, was offered a position on the Cincinnati Soccer Club staff.

Of any club I had previously coached for, I was very excited to become a part of. The level of community, integrity, and pure development of its players was something so beautiful I couldn't wait to get more involved. The philosophy of player development and the club's views aligned with mine, and it could not have been a better match-up.

When reflecting on my friendship with Nick, I remember all the games we attended together. When he watched those professional players, the fire in his eyes, the pure love for the game in every possible aspect, that is what I want for my players. I want that fire to burn in their body, and I want them to have a passion for the sport my friend loved so dearly. I want to not only make these kids I encounter on the pitch better soccer players, but I want to help mold and help them grow into good little humans. I want to teach them life lessons, and I want them to know all the good in life and remember to appreciate it when the bad storm waves hit.

This past year I had a player who lost her mother to cancer mid-season. I took on that loss as if it was my fault, even though it literally had nothing to do with me. I felt like I could have stopped it as if I had some sort of cancer-curing superpower. The guilt I felt for being alive. This family has two kids under ten years old who lost their mother and a devoted, loving father who lost his wife and best friend. That family will never be whole again. And I know that from experience. So, I did what I could to ease the pain of losing someone over the Christmas holidays and gathered donations from the Cincinnati Soccer Club community and got to play Santa Clause. I may not have been able to bring back their mother, but due to all those who pitched in, I was able to put a smile on those sweet kids' faces and relief to a grieving father and husband.

A few months later, our Spring season was getting ready to take off, and I held one of our first practices back at our indoor facility. At the end of practice, I called all my girls and sat down in a circle. I asked them all if they had a best friend and if they did to raise their hands. They all raised their hands, laughing and pointing at one another. I went on to tell them I had a best friend, and his name was Nick. I still, to this day, cannot say his name without feeling like I am fighting back the tears and choking on my words. These girls were so incredibly sweet and attentive in what I was saying and what points I was trying to get across. I went on to share Nick's battle with cancer, and they already knew I was a survivor. I explained grief and how difficult it is to lose someone you love, but that no matter what goes on in life, you will always have people who love you, and you will always have people around to lift you up.

This conversation was geared toward my player, who had just lost her mother, but it was a message I felt everyone needed to hear. When the conversation ended, I looked at every one of my players and told them If it was okay with them, I would like to dedicate this season in honor of her, her mother, and this player's entire family. The girls were all more than happy to do so. I had black memorial armbands embroidered with my player's mothers' initials in a beautiful cursive font in her favorite shade of purple. I slowly began to pass these out and looked over to find my player's face buried in her hands, knees to her chest, crying. I dismissed my team and scooted over to this sweet girl and just held her while she cried. I told her how much I loved her, how strong she is, how supported she is, and how much her mom loved her, and she would always be with her and to never forget that.

I hope I made a difference in this young girl's life. In her family's lives. Her father is one of my closest friends here in Cincinnati. I hold him and his family near and dear to my heart. Life experiences. Is it not crazy how our experiences in life often set us up to help others going through something similar? The knowledge we gain from our life experiences will always open up doors we never fathomed opening. Had I not gone through cancer, I would not have understood what my player's mom was fighting. Without experiencing so much loss, I would not have been able to empathize with this family. Without these experiences, I may not have been able to help and support them in the way I was willing and able to. Every winding road I decided to take, every door I opened and closed led me to these people.

CHAPTER SEVENTEEN

My Buoy

Now, October of 2019 had just rolled around, my sister-in-law Emily discovered I was newly single. Josh and Emily were getting married in Mexico in a few months, and Emily had two single friends coming that she thought I might be interested in. Now, this came as a shock to many people, but I hadn't dated men since high school. I'd honestly never been with a man, maybe because I knew I would never love anyone the way I loved Nick, or perhaps I was just meant to be with girls? Who knows? Now Emily went on to send me two pictures—one of a male who she was sure to inform me was a doctor, and one a female. Obviously, I was more intrigued by her female friend Heather. She gave me a brief biography of Heather, their friendship, and her life back in Kentucky. Oh yes, I said Kentucky. I decided to take a leap of faith, got Heather's contact information, and sent her a text.

I will never forget standing in the middle of my classroom during nap time and sending the first text, "Hi, this is Eileen Dowd. Your so-called best friend Emily is giving your number out like candy on Halloween." To my surprise, Heather responded, "Is this a trick or a treat?" And I think I knew right then and there I was going to be with that woman. The quick wit and back and forth banter was and will always be my favorite quality Nick possessed, and to my surprise, Heather and Nick shared that in common.

The months that followed were nothing but filled with love. Heather would fly to Texas; I would fly to Kentucky as we navigated a long-distance relationship. And not long after, COVID hit. I very quickly decided I was not going to go through quarantine alone. I was currently unhappy with teaching, so I decided to resign, pack my bags, and head to Kentucky for good. It was not until meeting Heather and then moving to Kentucky that I understood God's plan for me. You see, up to that point in my life, I always wondered why? Why did I have cancer? Why have I experienced so much loss? Within a few months of dating Heather, it was like everything had fallen into place. Every decision, every moment, every life experience set me up for meeting this beautiful human. Because of that realization, I made my peace with the Lord. I made peace with all the loss. I made peace with my life experiences.

You see, in previous relationships, it was as if I always had one foot out the door. But, with Heather, every day is filled with love and laughter. Arguments are talked through and resolved, and we tackle any issues that arise in life together. Heather is my "Buoy "when life feels tough or overwhelmed with everyday challenges; Heather is there to keep me above water steadily in a life filled with nothing but the unexpected. Heather is one of the best people I know, every trait and quality she possesses is good. Although she does what she can for others, she always carries a positive mindset in every possible situation.

In most relationships I had been in, there was always an expiration date. There were always bright, big lettered "Exit" signs beaming in the background telling me it was not going to work or that person was not for me. Not with Heather. From the moment I met her, I knew she was my forever person. On one of my first trips to Cincinnati, Heather took me to Devou Park. This Park is beyond my favorite to venture out to. On August 6, 2021, I planned a beautiful picnic for Heather and me. She had no idea; it was a surprise "date." Now five days prior, I had an indoor soccer game and ended up tearing ligaments in one of my ankles and was now in a big boot. Talk about the worst possible timing. Needless to say, I was not going to let this boot stop me from making one of the most significant decisions of my life. The nervous feeling, the anxiety in the pit of my stomach that was building as the weeks leading up to this sunny Friday evening. As I sat across from Heather, I looked at her sweet, beautiful face. It was at that moment I felt peace: no more nerves, no more anxiety. In that exact moment of time, I knew I was in the right place, with the right person and making the right decision.

I pulled three things out from behind my back—first, a dachshund ring dish. Heather used to have a miniature dachshund, Ollie, who she loved dearly. Next came a wooden card I had ordered from Etsy; on the front, it had a tree engraved with a heart in the middle of it; inside the heart, it read "ED+HD." When Heather turned it around, she read the words, "Want to keep the "D" and marry me?" Then, with tears in her eyes, she picked her head up, and we locked eyes both with smiles on our faces, and thankfully, she said yes. Heather is now my fiancé and my forever person.

CHAPTER EIGHTEEN

Still Water

My relationship with God slowly became non-existent as I watched children suffer from cancer or have to be placed in either urn or caskets. I couldn't understand the reasoning behind it all. Why? That's all I could ask, why? Why are they gone? Why did I beat cancer, and they didn't? What purpose do I have that they couldn't have carried out?

I stopped turning to God. I stopped praying for an extended period of time. But then, I met a girl at school before Nick died, her name was Kassie. Kassie was so good to me throughout, having to see me suffer through the loss of Nick. I will never forget her telling me whenever I feel sad or alone to say these eight words, "Be still and know that I am God." To this day, when I'm feeling down, I repeat those eight words, and I always think of what a dear friend she was to me at that time in my life.

God has a reason. God has a plan. Both statements I have heard over a million times throughout my life. I could have punched every person who said that to me square in the face. But now, at this point in my life, I get it. I see the plan; I know the reasoning. I finally understand. You see, we are all individuals on our own paths navigating through life. Life is like a wave, with highs and lows and events like an undertow that will just wipe you right off your feet. You have to ride out the highs, ride out the lows and avoid being sucked into that current. I was sick for a reason, and I survived for a reason. I have a higher purpose in this world, and I have a message to share.

I firmly believe everything does happen for a reason. People are placed in our lives for a reason. It is our job here on earth to make a difference. We go through these life experiences, some good and some bad. And I believe we go through these obstacles to learn lessons, and with those life lessons, we can then move forward and help others. With all that I have learned, my mission is to spread faith, hope, and love to all those I cross paths with. Trust that God has a plan, hope that anything is achievable, and show love to all. At the end of the day, what are we without those three things?

Chapter Nineteen

Tranquil Water

"When we touch peace, everything becomes real."

—Thich Nhat Hanh

＊ ＊ ＊ ＊ ＊

Peace—the freedom of disturbance. It took over ten years to make peace with the events that have occurred in my life. The trauma, the repressed memories, the events that shaped me into the human being I am today. For ten years, I mourned the loss of so many people in my life. For ten years, I lived with an unspeakable amount of guilt and sadness—the lack of understanding of God's plan. I was like someone who was in prison, a mental prison; after ten years, I was free of my sentence.

I used to always hear, "time heals all wounds." I hated hearing those four words. I wanted to slap anyone who said that to me. To me, time does not heal all wounds—or any wounds at all. All time does is allow you to reflect, remember and move on the best you can. Time has allowed me to reflect on all the memories made with my dear friends. Time has allowed me to remember the good, the bad, and the unbearable. Time has allowed me to see what those memories mean. Meaning, the bad memories have made me appreciative of the good memories. The agonizing memories have prepared me for the challenging moments I will encounter in the future.

You see, every moment in your life is preparing you for something bigger. In my case, my life has prepared me in a way to help others in many forms. I am able to empathize and relate to a broad group of people. People fighting cancer, survivors of cancer, people dealing with grief, people within the LGBTQ community, and being a positive role model for children I encounter on and off the soccer field.

When you are able to find peace in your life, when you are able to accept the devastation, the successes, and the unexplainable—it is in that exact moment you are then able to use the lessons learned in life to pay it forward to others. In my eyes and through my experiences, that is what life is all about. Helping others get through the crazy tsunami we call life. Ride the waves alongside others and bring them to the calm waters of tranquility.

* * * * *

"Our true home is in the present moment. To live in the present moment is a miracle. The miracle is not to walk on water. The miracle is to walk on the green Earth in the present moment, to appreciate the peace and beauty that are available now. Peace is all around us—in the world and in nature——and within us—in our bodies and our spirits. Once we learn to touch this peace, we will be healed and transformed."[4]

* * * * *

Some nights, some mornings, I lay in bed and think about my life, how much I have endured, how much I have had to overcome, and how much I have had to overcome. Life is all about finding a

---

4   Hạnh *Touching Peace*, 1.

little piece of Heaven here on earth. Being able to find happiness within oneself is the greatest accomplishment of all. To not depend on any, one person or any one thing. To just find pure peace and happiness within. Persevere against all odds stacked up against you. My dad used to always tell me, well, he still does tell me, "Through perseverance comes strength." I now know what that means. Those four words could not be more accurate. I am who I am today because of what I have been through. I am stronger because of my past traumas. Whatever any one person is going through in life, persevere. Loss is part of life; it is inevitable. It will break your heart. It will rip your world apart. It is the way we approach the waves of life that will define us. Will you ride the waves? Will you get sucked under the undertow? You decide the paths you take in this world. I did not write this book because I think I am extraordinary; I always thought you definitely had to be someone special to write or even publish a book. I wrote this book to share my story, my life struggles, and my victories. I wrote this book to show even though I was drowning for the longest time, that the ocean had literally swallowed me whole and spit me back out multiple times, calmer waters always come. It takes time; for me, it took a long while. But the clear waters are well worth the wait.

Epilogue

The year 2020 was and will always be the happiest year of my life. I found true love, moved across the country, and made a name for myself in a new city where I knew no one. Today you can often find me out on the soccer fields all around the Ohio area. I coach multiple youth soccer teams for Cincinnati Soccer Club. I also had the opportunity to Nanny for the most beautiful family, who I remain very close to and consider family.

I am a full-time student at a local college where I am working towards a degree in Exercise Science to continue my coaching career. My education has always been something I believed to be unachievable and one of my biggest regrets. However, as I have gotten older and more time has gone by to give my brain time to heal, I was finally confident enough to re-enroll and get back to it. To my surprise, my memory has improved, and I am more than happy to report I am excelling in all my classes.

As for my personal life, Heather is still perfectly imperfect. On days I don't have classes or soccer, you can find the two of us spending time with our three fur babies, Charlie, Carter, and Reagan. Heather is someone who supports me in everything I do, my biggest cheerleader, and the best friend I could have. She is someone with an open mind, always willing to give advice, and holds my hand through all of life's successes and challenges. We plan to have a wedding in 2023 surrounded by all our family and loved ones.

My family has and will always be so incredibly important to me. I will carry the guilt I feel with my past actions and what I have put each of them through as individuals and as a family with me for the rest of my life. But I am happy to say the relationships with my brothers and parents have improved immensely. My mother is my best friend, my dad is my most significant source of support, Anthony is always there when I need him, Josh is always there to give wisdom, and sweet Jake is always there to keep me laughing. This is my family. These five outstanding individuals are who I get to call family. I am blessed.

With all this being said, my life is not perfect by any means. There are days I still struggle, and there are days I don't get out of bed. But for the most part, I have found peace, I have found happiness, and I have come to an understanding of my life struggles. My counselor, Becks, always said to me, *"Live a life worth living,"* and with confidence, I can say I am living a life worth living. Furthermore, I am living a life I am proud of.

THE WARRIOR

Gazing in the mirror,
I see a woman's face.
Fully clothed in armor,
No fear and no disgrace.

A tear it never offers,
A smile it always gives.
No sadness does it show,
But what a life it lives.

Needles going in
As blood is taken out,
But still no sign of pain,
No cries to make you doubt.

Each day you see this person,
And think that they're so brave,
Each day you see us laughing,
The tears are ours to save.

So when you see our armor,
And think that we're calm and mild,
Remember this one thing,
The warrior is a child.

Written by Terra Phillips

Eileen and Nick

Jazmin & Eileen (2yrs) 1995

Eileen and Jazmin

Eileen and Corina

Dowd Family

Eileen and Lilli

Eileen and Heather

Eileen Coaching and playing soccer

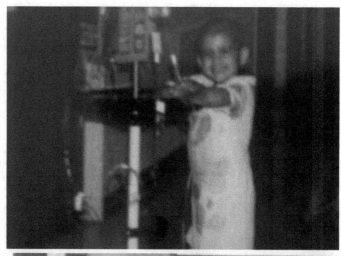

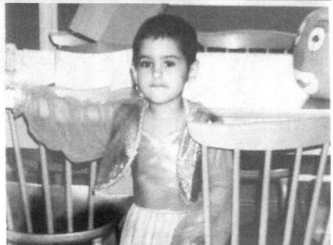

Eileen in treatment

Eileen and Freddy